Wellbeing 17

D1465355

914NR

First Published 2018

by John Catt Educational Limited
15 Riduna Park, Station Road,
Melton, Woodbridge IP12 1QT
Tel: +44 (0) 1394 389850 Fax: +44 (0) 1394 386893
Email: enquiries@johncatt.com
Website: www.johncatt.com

ISBN: 978 1 911382 73 7

Set and designed by John Catt Educational Limited.

Contents

The 25 Careers

INTRODUCTION

This book is an unapologetic millennial manifesto for career happiness. Too many of us are unhappy in what we do for a living and that needs to change.

This is a book for you if you grew up not having the faintest clue what to do with your life. You drifted through the education system and when it got to your final year, you panicked. You applied for 37 different jobs in nearly as many different industries and you accepted the first job offer you got. Turns out you don't like this one so much. You have a few years' experience in it now, but are still no closer to figuring out what you would really like to do than when you were aged nine.

Now you feel trapped.

This is a book for you if you grew up knowing exactly what you wanted to do. You might have spent years of your life training for it and thousands of pounds paying for that education. Then you finally got there. Turns out that it isn't the golden career you thought it was. Turns out you were wrong, and this isn't your life's dream after all.

Now you feel trapped.

You might be at the tail end of the millennial generation, at the beginning of one of those paths, having only just graduated, for example, or you might be much further along and have over a decade of experience in your field. The feelings are the same though – you feel trapped. You don't feel in control of your own career path, not really.

You are questioning if this is really what life is all about. You don't want to just live for the weekend; really you want to be embracing every single day of your life. You know that money is important, but you also know that it can only bring you so much. Happiness isn't the same thing as security and stability. You feel unfulfilled, restless and fed up.

Something needs to change.

This is not a book that will give you all the answers, but it will ask you the right questions and help you to figure out the answers for yourself. The questions in this book aren't rhetorical – write down your answers as you go. They are there to help you figure out exactly what it is you want to do and to gain some career clarity.

You probably already know some of the answers deep down; you might have just forgotten them because you were seven years old when you figured them out, instead of 24 or 34.

When you are seven and someone tells you that being a video game designer is a ridiculous idea and isn't a real job, you believed them and tried to forget about it. Or there might have always been two or three things that you have longed to do and even though you may have picked one of those, not being able to explore the other two things has left you feeling unfulfilled in the career that you do have. It is even perfectly possible that your dream job just didn't exist when you were growing up, or that you never knew what all the options were until it was 'too late'.

I hear you and I have been there. Except, I have come out the other side. I had a major quarter life crisis. So major that I quit my job and spent a year trying out 25 different careers before my 25th birthday.

The jobs I tried ranged from archaeology in Transylvania, tour guiding amid violent protests in Venezuela and investigative journalism with a national newspaper, to working as an extra in a major movie, alpaca farming in Cornwall and assisting a crisis team during the terror attack on Parliament in March 2017. All of that work experience worked.

Expert opinions, research and interviews will be combined with the anecdotal experience that comes from trying so many jobs, to help us deal with and understand the bigger picture of what's going on: why are so many of us unhappy? What can we do about it, both on an individual level and as a wider generational workforce who are on the cusp of taking on senior positions?

Chapter One will focus on what it's like to hate your job, looking at the months leading up to that quarter life crisis tipping point, as well as examining the extent of the problem and showing that you are not alone. It will talk about smashed avocados and how economic factors far beyond our control are trapping us in a system where the only thing we do have control over is our aim for happiness at work.

Chapter Two covers what you should do when it all gets too much and you reach that quarter-life crisis trigger moment. It will look at how you deal with the emotional fall-out and how you can weigh up your career options when you don't know what you want to do. It highlights the importance of work experience at any age and will then go into detail about how I ended up trying 25 different jobs – and how you could too.

Chapter Three discusses how to go about crafting your own path by looking at why you are unhappy in the first place, what sort of things you might want out of your career and finding the right working environment for you.

Chapter Four is all about networking as a means of getting both work experience placements and jobs. It will walk you through how to go about getting 25 different work placements in a year and be a boss at networking, including how to use social media to your advantage, how to find your way around networking events and access the hidden jobs market.

Chapter Five focuses on the reality of a career change and exploring your options through work experience, by examining how you find the time and the money to practically implement some of the ideas discussed in previous chapters.

Chapter Six presents a solution by explaining the concept of portfolio careers, delving into why they are such a good idea and exactly how you can go about creating your own. It will also divulge exactly what I did next.

Finally, Chapter Seven brings it all together as part of a bigger picture. It advocates for real change in the world of work, to a focus on fulfilment and being future-facing. It is a call-to-action, arguing that we, as a generation, must embrace our expectations in order to build a workplace that moves beyond the persistent industrial revolution approach to one appropriate for the digital revolution.

This is a book that will challenge and disrupt every assumption you've ever had about your place in the world of work and will guide you through a new type of careers education, where you determine your own journey. It might even inspire you to take your own radical sabbatical.

CHAPTER ZERO POINT FIVE

ON LOVING
YOUR JOB

That Sunday night feeling. The euphoric adrenaline rush of what the next day will hold, you can barely sleep from the excitement. Your heart is pounding as you go through all the possible scenarios, palms sweating at the desperation of wanting to do well and for everything to go your way. There is a nervous but quiet confidence at the back of your mind telling you that you can do this, you know you can do this. Tomorrow, you will be the best version of yourself that you can be. There will be validation of that from those who know you best, those whose opinions you care most about.

You check the time. Only two minutes have passed since you last looked. You wish you could sleep because that would mean the morning would be here sooner. But it evades you, the buzz of what comes next is too much to ignore. You chant 'sleep, sleep, sleep' to yourself to try and override the thrilling inner-monologue. Slowly, it begins to work and the gentle waves of drowsiness take charge, pulling you off.

Your dreams are filled with what had just been your waking thoughts, and the fear of being late. You are restless, tossing and turning for hours. When you are finally awoken in the morning, you are drained and your mind is hazy. It takes a few seconds for you to remember why you feel this way. It pings back into your consciousness sharply; you are amazed you ever forgot.

You qualify as a doctor and will save someone's life today.

Today you will get your first class of children as a new teacher.

You will defend an innocent person in court for the first time today, seeing justice done.

You are an Olympic athlete and today is the big race.

This is the day your first book will be launched.

You announce your discovery of a step towards a cancer cure to the world today.

Tonight, you will give your first performance as a prima ballerina.

You get to take your first flight as the pilot of a Boeing-747.

You will enter Earth's orbit for the first time, joining the International Space Station.

It's the day your career really starts.

CHAPTER ONE

ON HATING YOUR JOB

to millennials:
twenty years from now you will be more disappointed by the things
you didn't do than by the ones you did do. so throw off the bowlines.
sail away from the safe harbour.
– mark twain

to our elders, with respect:
we often refuse to accept an idea merely because the tone of
voice in which it has been expressed is unsympathetic to us.
– friedrich nietzsche

That Sunday night feeling. Lying awake, despondently counting down the hours until I would have to go to work in the morning brought the familiar tight knot of stress in my chest. I kept making mental lists of everything I had to do but didn't want to do the next day. I could hardly quit my job, that's not what people do when they have the long-term job security offered by the public sector I worked in. Besides, think of the pension.

There are so many rational reasons to stay in a job: salary, stability, and career progression. If you are a young person, particularly, you are usually 'very lucky to be here' and you should be 'grateful for this fantastic opportunity'.

Except, life doesn't always work like that. Just because it makes sense, because it is rational, it doesn't make it any easier for us to want to get up when our alarm goes off at half past six on a Monday morning, or Tuesday morning, or even Wednesday. We hit snooze and doze for another ten minutes, not out of laziness, but because we want to do something, anything, other than face the day ahead. We imagine what it might be like if we wanted to get up and go to work. We assume **someone**, some lucky person out there, must surely get to skip off to work every day and feel fulfilled, satisfied, and ultimately happy at the prospect of what awaits them?

After another two, maybe three, snooze-slams, we drag ourselves out of the warm safety of bed and drowsily plod off to the bathroom, knowing we cannot really call in for another sickie. A Monday morning sickie is too obvious anyway.

We have all had those days, weeks, even those months or years. But how do we begin to separate a bad day from a bad job? What is a normal level of dissatisfaction and disengagement from our careers? Isn't this just how life works, we ask ourselves? All the negative connotations that come from the word 'work' are there for a reason, it is not meant to be a pleasant thing to do.

Deep down, though, we know this probably isn't true. We question if this is something we tell ourselves because it helps to normalise how we feel and block out the thoughts of negativity, at least until next Sunday evening. Besides, we ask, what would we realistically do instead? Our CVs are often tailored to the next career move on the path we are already on. Some of us have degrees, professional qualifications or even several years of specific experience that encourage us to keep doing what we are doing; to change that we would have to start again, all the way at the bottom. This in itself is a terrifying thought, let alone if you consider the rent or mortgage and bills, maybe even the child, that depends on your salary.

It leaves us feeling trapped. Constricted. The four walls are closing in around us. The nagging doubts of whether this is our lot in life, if this is what we were truly meant to do or if we are just settling, never quite leave us. Some of us hit our 40s or 50s and make radical decisions, perhaps we buy garishly coloured convertibles, get a tattoo or have a sudden urge to go to a nightclub and order massively overpriced bottles of champagne, despite the fact that we now get a really bad headache after just two glasses.

This crisis is not age dependant, though. For many, it hits earlier rather than later. For many, it hits in the years shortly after getting our first job. For many, it hits in our 20s and early 30s.

We don't really talk about it when we have a crisis that young – it sounds too disingenuous. We fear our elders will mock us, and that's only because we **are** routinely mocked by many of our elders. We read media article after article that tells us that we are spoiled millennials. We are told that if we would only stop buying avocados, then all our problems will go away. Smash.

It's working. Like feminists afraid of identifying with their own label, so too are many millennials attempting to dissociate themselves from their own generational nickname; we don't want to get drawn into the perceived murk and difficulty of the term that we should unashamedly own.

We are only allowed to hate our jobs once we have suffered

through them for another 20 years, don't you know? Hating your job after only two or three years means you need to suffer more. We are disloyal. We are ungrateful. We are selfish. We are snowflakes. All because we don't want to live the same life that our parents did.

As a generation, we are crying out for a change from the way things have always been done. We just don't want to do it anymore.

The world of work as it stood in the 1960s, '70s, '80s, '90s and even the 2000s no longer exists. The nature of work has changed beyond recognition with technology as its linchpin. Except, the way we think about work hasn't caught up and our expectations from it are at odds with that change, depending on our generational perspective.

We are offered pacifiers like office beanbags, table top football and work-at-home-Fridays, because that will make a workplace 'millennial friendly'. Often, we meekly accept these as fair compromises even though they don't really address the crux of the problem.

When I say that I hated my path in life at age 24 and decided I wanted to do something about it, some will slam this book shut in disgust.

Oh please, a young person having an existential crisis? Grow up. Live another 20 years in that job and then have your crisis. Your feelings do not matter. You are too young to be taken seriously.

Except the person 20 years older than our critics laughs down on that view. Our grandparents' generation mocked our parents' generation just the same, as did our great-grandparents to our grandparents, as we will to our children.

When they are young, each generation has it 'the hardest it's ever been'. Each generation rebels in their own way. And the generation above hates them all the same. Baby boomers had their Summer of Love; we are now trying to get through a Winter of Discontent. Even now, we wonder what those who have grown up swiping an iPad before learning to speak in full sentences will be like when they get to working age. What will they change when they arrive?

It is too simplistic of a view to pick up this book and think it is about another young person moaning about their job. No. This book wants to change the way things are done, because being miserable in your job should not be the norm, and for too many of us it is. Maybe the commute-9-to-5-commute routine isn't getting the best out of us. Maybe the system needs updating to reflect the world we now live in and everyone in it, including those who will soon begin to lead us through the next great wave of societal changes. If you are a young person reading this, then you probably already know that: you know something needs to change.

We were raised in an education system created and designed during the Industrial Revolution, not the Information Revolution. We learned traditional subjects and public exams were memory tests; at its heart, learning by rote was valued over learning by imagination, innovation or fostering a natural curiosity. Those were coincidental by-products.

But it is things like creativity and innovation that will make us resilient in the workplace in the decades to come. These are skills that technology is much less likely to be able to independently do. What use is advanced mental arithmetic when we have calculators on the phones that never leave our sides?

Our careers education too was one-dimensional. Tick the boxes in the multiple-choice personality test and it will spit you out your answer. There. Problem solved. When we were teenagers, very little about careers education had changed since the days of *Monty Python's* Vocational Guidance Counsellor sketch. You can find it quite easily on the internet, though it starts like this:

Counsellor: And now, Mr Anchovy, you asked us to advise you which job in life you were best suited for.

Anchovy: That is correct, yes.

Counsellor: Well I now have the results here of the interviews and the aptitude tests that you took last week, and from them we have built up a pretty clear picture of the sort of person that you are. And I think

I can say, without fear of contradiction, that the ideal job for you is chartered accountancy.

Anchovy: But I am a chartered accountant.

Counsellor: Jolly good. Well back to the office with you then.

Anchovy: No! No! No! You don't understand... I want a new job. Something exciting that will let me live.

Does this sound familiar?

It was recorded in 1969. That's 50 years ago exactly to this book's publication.

When it comes to our career choices, we have been raised on the same set of mantras that are preached as universal, unchallengeable truths while growing up.

Do what you are good at when you were at school. Do what earns you the most money. Do what will make your parents proud. Do the job that gives you security. Do what will get you promoted.

Follow the path we have laid out for you. Be logical. Be realistic.

That's not a real job. You can't earn a living doing that. How will you provide for your hypothetical future family?

But you are good at [school subject], so you should do that. Be like your slightly older and always more perfect family member. Be serious.

The noise is overwhelming and all consuming. We were young and eager to please. We gave in, consciously or subconsciously, and said yes. Now we are living out our parents' dreams. Dreams that were relevant 20 or 30 years ago but no longer have to be.

But, did anyone ever ask: what makes you happy? Are you happy now? No? No one asked me neither.

That doesn't mean that things can't change though; the feeling of being trapped does not necessarily mean that you actually are. That's why you are reading this book.

I followed the path. I ticked all the boxes. I got good grades at school, not through natural academic talent but through a combination of hard work, good role models and happening to fall into the 'right' demographic categories. I applied to university, because that was what you do. I went to university and again, I worked hard to do well and was expected to do well. I started to see life as a game you had to play, and I wanted to win, or more importantly, I didn't want to lose. The fear of failure can be equally as good of an incentive as the pressure of success; as can wanting to prove your naysayers wrong.

To do well at The Game of Life you follow the pre-ordained path:

Step One: You get good grades at school and get into university.

Step Two: You get good grades at university, and then you do some extra-curricular activities and get an internship, because the combination of the above is how you get a job.

Step Three: You apply to 30 different jobs, and you get rejected from 29 of them. When one says yes, you don't hesitate. You say 'thank you very much' and seal it with a virtual handshake. You start to earn a salary.

Step Four: If all goes well (as you and everyone else expect it to) then you get a small pay rise or promotion after a year or two. You are now able to rent a slightly nicer flat that finally looks better maintained than your student house. You may even get a new job with a different company within the same industry.

Step Five: Eventually, you earn enough to buy your first home, probably when you have a partner who also has a reasonable salary so that you can split the deposit. You move in, hopefully coupled with a promotion at work to make the mortgage a little easier. And so life goes on.

True, no one might have laid it out in quite such precise terms, but they never really needed to because you already knew that this was the case, this was what life was going to look like. If you played the game as you should have, then you would be 'successful' and live happily ever after.

This model of life is black and white. It leaves no room for shades of grey. It might allow small deviances such as inserting 'Step 1B: A Gap Year', but that's about it. Once you start work in your first adult job, there are no professional shades of grey. Very occasionally, an acquaintance of yours or your sister's boyfriend's second cousin's neighbour might change career, but it is always someone else and it is relatively risk-free – from one safe job to another, perhaps with a small amount of re-training. They will sure as hell know that there will be a secure job waiting for them on the other side.

Hypothetically, we know that having more than one career across our working lives is not unusual; there are plenty of reports that we will change careers at least five times.[1] That knowledge doesn't always provide comfort, however, as it still feels abstract and unobtainable, particularly if you are without role models who are only a phone call away. You have made a mistake in your career choice once before, how do you know you won't make the same mistake twice, possibly putting you in an even worse position than you are in now?

Forever a 'good girl', I didn't consider anything other than a traditional career path, intending on choosing one direction and sticking with it until the very end. I followed the game to the letter. I got to around Step Four and was doing well. I got my Bachelor's degree and then won a scholarship to study for my Master's; I had my what I thought was my dream job.

I then managed to get a job offer on a competitive public sector graduate scheme. This was a job that made sense. It led straight on from my degrees. It would set me up for life. I would be able to help people and make our country a better place, one little step at a time. That's all I really wanted to do – help people. Idealistic and naive, absolutely, but if you aren't able to be those things when you are 22, then when?

I was dealt a lucky hand at birth. Statistically speaking, I was more likely than most to win at life's game before I had even learnt to crawl. I was born into a white, middle class family in a Greater London suburb. Both my parents are still happily married to each other. They both had well-paid jobs while I was growing up. They provided me with a stable, supportive and loving home life and were able to send me to a good school. The path had been paved for me to have all the opportunities possible so that I could have the best possible chance of winning too.

Joining the public sector was my way of giving back to those who hadn't been as lucky through no fault of their own. I wanted other people to not have to be so dependent on being dealt a good hand when growing up. I felt and still strongly feel that life should be what we as individuals make of it – we should all be able to begin at the same start line. Opportunity shouldn't just be for the few.

On starting work, a healthy dose of realism quickly followed. That idealistic light rapidly dimmed and routine and drudgery flourished.

The issues that I was working on sounded fascinating and fulfilling in equal measure on paper. In reality, there was no distinction between my jobs in terms of what day-to-day life was like. Every day involved commuting with my nose in someone's armpit for two hours a day (genuinely – I am 5'1"), sitting at a desk, in front of a computer and coming home again, and again, and again.

They could have been desk jobs anywhere, on any issue. There were a couple of hundred emails a day, a smattering of rushed meetings and phone calls, and leagues of inefficient bureaucracy. It involved being entirely sedentary with no daylight or fresh air – all day, every day. In winter, I would arrive at work in the dark and leave that evening in the dark, having ticked off a few more boxes on my to-do list. The routine and inactivity of daily life was something I was completely unable to move past, a feeling that no brisk lunchtime walk could alleviate.

Was I really helping others? No. If I continued down the path I had chosen for another 15 or 20 years then I **may** have been senior enough to have **some** impact. Maybe. If there coincidentally happened to be political will around an issue at the same time I was working on it.

Was I adding value to the organisations I was working for at least? Not much. Would I have had the opportunity to in a few years, once I had learnt my craft and had 'done my time' at the bottom? From the endless networking coffees that I'd had with those more senior to me, the answer was no, not really.

So what was I doing, staring at the beige, picture-less wall behind my computer screen? The older colleagues sitting next to me often said how they were just riding it out until retirement. The nagging doubts of whether this is our lot in life couldn't be placated. It struck me as such a waste of life.

I was becoming increasingly disillusioned. Why had everyone lied about the Game of Life? The game made me feel claustrophobic, trapped, with a knot of stress constantly squeezing my stomach, chest, throat.

The game was shit.

But on you persevere, because that is what you do. That is just what the world of work is.

Why, though? Why is this just what the world of work is?

Why do 72% of us millennials want to change career completely? Cross-generationally, it's 54%.

44% of the workforce is completely disengaged from their job.[234] But on we persevere.

To give more context, in the UK that is ten million millennials who want to change career and over 17 million across the workforce as a whole.[56] 14 million are disengaged.[7] But we keep calm and carry on.

That is an almost incomprehensibly large number, and this is just for our small island alone, of which you and I are just two. These statistics are from the conservative studies; some research goes as far as to say that only 13% of the global population 'actually like going to work'.[8] What are the rest of us? Ambivalent at best and outright miserable at worst?

The knowledge you are not alone is comforting. Whilst it may feel like you are the only person who feels the way you do, it's vital to listen to the more rational voice in your head. Have courage in your convictions.

Being desperately unhappy in your job is an isolating experience. Often difficult to express to friends or family, we are convinced we should just grin and bear it, perhaps even considering ourselves weak or feeling guilty for questioning the status quo. Part of the problem is that we do not know what we would do instead. Admitting that you want to leave your job to move into another is much easier to say than you want to quit with a dramatic blaze of glory mic drop that is worthy of the front page of Reddit, damning all consequences.

Changing jobs within the same industry is the status quo; it is pretty safe and predictable. Taking a completely different path into the directionless unknown, however, is terrifying, possibly even foolhardy.

Realising you are not alone is an uplifting first step towards pragmatically addressing the issue of identifying exactly why you are ambivalent at best and outright miserable at worst. Worry about the why before you consider what you should do about it.

One of the main reasons for writing this book is so that you know that you are not alone.

I hadn't yet realised that, at this point though. Instead, I had started to notice all the small bad things, and fewer of the small good things in life. Every time someone sneezed over me on the tube. Every time my computer froze. Every time I sat in a meeting and realised it was totally unnecessary. Every time I was copied in on an email that bore no relevance to what I was working on. Every time I ate a soggy sandwich for lunch. Every time the sun left the edge of my desk after staying for just half an hour. Every time the 18:34 train home was delayed because there was a leaf on the tracks. Every time someone told me how lucky I was to be there.

Each day consisted of a growing number of small frustrations. These were useful in a way, as they distracted me from what was the real problem; that I hated what my life was becoming. There was an on-going battle in my head. I had done everything right, ticked every box and I was winning at that game, so why was I so miserable?

There were countless nights that I lay awake staring and the ceiling and dreading my alarm. There were nights that I was in tears, distraught with disappointment at myself, feeling selfish and ungrateful for not wanting to grab every opportunity with the enthusiasm I had once had, and undeserving of where I was now. I started cancelling plans with friends at the last minute, not wanting to face social situations because I had gotten myself so worked up. There were Saturday nights where I drank too much, partly to forget about the situation, only to discover it rushing back to me once I was at peak drunkenness. Friends and family noticed the change, but I pushed them away because I couldn't talk about it, I didn't want to admit that I was a failure for wanting to reject my 'perfect' career.

The Game of Life wasn't working for me. I had everything material that I needed and wanted; I also had status and respect from friends and family. I was right on track. But every single day, I paused outside my office's front door and closed my eyes, taking a deep, long, sinking breath and imagined that I was somewhere else, before continuing with my stride.

Was this it? Was this what winning at life felt like?

I sheepishly started to look for other jobs within my sector, hoping my job was the problem rather than my career or something altogether deeper than that, and sent out plenty of ill-thought-through applications. I didn't get any of them – I was more focused on what I **didn't** want than what I **did** want, and my applications reflected this sentiment of desperation, rather than that of serious professionalism. Constant rejections only made the situation worse.

So, I limped on distractedly for a few months more.

We are now working hard to stop telling our children to 'man up', but it is still readily acceptable, encouraged even, to tell our younger workforce to 'man up' and just get on with their job.[9] Feeling deeply unhappy, anxious or even formal anxiety and depression are seen as less acceptable if they are triggered by issues in the workplace, because 'it's normal, no one actually likes their job'. Or at least, 87% of us don't.

People respond to these feelings in different ways. Some of us isolate ourselves further, lacking the energy to do anything when we do have free time after work and on weekends. We can shut ourselves away at home, stewing on how life could be different, not wanting to share concerns with our friends or family. We can become tense, lashing out at those who care most about us. That Sunday night dread can become an ever-present weight on our shoulders, dragging us down. It grinds you down, tugging at the corners of our mouths, making life one long grimace between the hours of nine and five.

Others of us react by doing the inverse. We are the ones that will go out every night after work and every Friday and Saturday, spending all day Sunday in a deep hangover, recovering from the lack of sleep, and the alcohol and possibly drugs surging through our veins from the exhausting week we have just had. We are the ones who are antagonising ourselves, continuously picking at and pushing our limits, unsure of how far we can stretch them and bend their rules. The problem arises when this is every single week. We often do this so we don't have to think about the problem. We make sure we are as busy as we can possibly be; we bury it. We cannot allow ourselves to stop and think for a breath because we are a little bit worried about what we will be like if we take ownership of our feelings.

These are two more extreme examples of how we may react when we aren't happy at work (or in other areas of life). Yet, different degrees of each, or sometimes a combination of the two, are what torments us out of fear of what we may find if we waver from our personal party lines.

It was only after I started fully expressing my concerns in conversations with friends and family that it became clear that I wasn't the only one – many of them did too. In typical British fashion with our top lips stiff and sturdy, we just hadn't had a serious conversation about it before.

If you have felt 'meh' about your job, avoid the subject when someone asks about your day, or when cornered by friends in the pub, you say that 'it's not that bad, it's just a job' – it doesn't have to be that way.

This book has been written specifically to give practical and realistic guidance on how to manoeuvre yourself out of that situation and into a new one that you are fully in control of. Because being 'just OK' shouldn't be OK.

In my life, though, I wasn't really even OK. Taking a week's annual leave for a Mediterranean summer holiday was the trigger for change. It was the first proper break I'd had in nearly a year and so was the first chance I'd had to take a step back to reflect. Except, I couldn't focus on the sun or sea, I was struggling to live in the moment and kept finding my trail of thought spiralling down into the dark cave that was facing me on return to the office.

What was going on? I would just have to do better on my job applications until I was successful. What more was there to this? I had been working there for a year, so moving in the next few months wouldn't be too bad. I had the very common problem of hating my job so I would get a new one, simple.

Except, the more I followed that path in my head, the less it felt like the right decision. It didn't seem like it would make me feel any better than I did now. I started digging deeper; I didn't like what I found just below the surface. Both at the situation and even more so at myself there was anger; resentment; frustration; guilt; fear. My sense of self-worth had reached its lowest trough – I told myself that I was like a spoilt and impertinent child who was throwing away opportunity that I should be desperate to hold on to. I was infantilising myself, believing that I must be incapable of mature and rational thought if that was the way I felt.

There must be something wrong with me, normal people don't get this worked up over not liking their job – they just got on with it. I concluded that I should consider therapy.

The days in the sun ticked by and on the last afternoon, as I was about to leave the poolside to start packing and, holding onto the steps of the swimming pool, I burst into tears at the thought of going back to work. Not just a few tears of self-pity. It was an involuntary response to the internal monologue that I'd been trying to silence for nearly a year. It was an uncontrollable outburst of raw emotion. I was choking on a mixture of my own tears and snotty phlegm. I felt like a pathetic mess. I couldn't push it back into its little box any longer. I had a bit of an emotional breakdown, in my soggy bikini in full view of the general public and any passers-by who cared to stop and stare.

Humiliated and dripping my way over to an already damp towel, I decided that it was enough. I refused to go on like this. In theory I had a lot to lose, but anything was far better than how this felt, I would figure out the practicalities later. So rather, it felt like I had nothing to lose. I was going to quit, end of story – job lined up or not.

Right then, the knowledge that I was going to quit my job was enough, it didn't really matter what I was going to do instead or how I would financially support myself. That I had made the decision to leave had lifted enough weight to allow me to pull myself together enough to gather up my things and squelch off to shower.

How had things gotten to that point? How had they gotten so bad?

Much of it centred around the yawning gap between my expectations on entering the workforce and the reality.

We, as millennials, want it all and we have been raised to fully expect it all; except our expectations are dramatically failing to match up to the reality of a post-recession world. Whilst our job market has bounced back, with the employment rate at a record high, our wages are stagnant, declining year-on-year in real terms. For one of the first times, 'low wages now explain low unemployment, rather than low unemployment acting as a catalyst for better pay'.[10][11] We as employees no longer have the bargaining power.

Job stability was the Holy Grail of our parents' generation, and with that came the benefits of financial security, home ownership and a relatively affordable cost of living. The message of 'aim to achieve job stability and personal prosperity will follow' is one we were raised on, watching the enticing success of our Baby Boomer and Generation X parents. Indeed, our start in life was more privileged than any previous generation due to the relative stability and wealth that our parents were able to offer, and we had expectations to match when we entered the workforce. But on entering the workforce in our 20s and as we move into our 30s, we have gone from being the most privileged to the least – we are now the first generation in recorded British history to be worse off than our parents.

In times gone by, there existed an unspoken social contract between employers and employees; play the game. Work hard and you will be rewarded by earning more each year. Your time in the office earns you enough to buy a home and start a family, fulfilling your dreams and desires in your personal life. The professional funded the personal, so it was all worthwhile.

Today, however, that trade-off is gone. When we work hard to gain our qualifications in school, college and university and are then lucky enough to gain one of the elusive stable office jobs, we no longer reap the rewards.

House prices have increased at a far greater rate than salaries; our salaries will no longer buy us a home.

The average millennial will pay £44,000 more in rent than our parents by our 30th birthdays, and home ownership by that age has fallen 21% between our two generations, at a conservative estimate.[12] If we are lucky, our salaries will buy us 25% of a home when we reach out mid-30s, or a home without a living room or one that is dependent on us continuing to have a partner or reliance on the Bank of Mum and Dad.[13]

The Bank of Mum and Dad, or BOMAD as it has been acronymised, is the ninth largest lender in the UK, with over £6.5bn in loans going to their children.[14] The scale of BOMAD in particular shows us that something has changed; something is not working in our system as our young people try to transition into the total independence of adulthood.

Whilst such generosity is something that our generation is incredibly grateful for, it leaves us dependant on our parents for vastly longer than ever before. It is also dependant on us having parents who are fortunate enough to be able to subsume such a high level of financial commitment and risk later in life, with long saved for pensions often liable. For millennials who are reliant on this, it only further entrenches feelings of being trapped by the responsibility many of us will have to our parents and their magnanimity – emotionally, financially or most probably both.[15]

A graph that was published by The Guardian in February 2016 clearly illustrates the gradual rise in private renting over the years in adults under 35 as the decline of home owning continues. By 2012/2013 53.5% of UK low to middle income households were private renters while 25.3% were homeowners. This is a dramatic reverse from the year 1996/1997 where approximately 20% of households were renting and 55% were homeowners. [16]

This pushes us into a form of prolonged adolescence that means we are always dependant on others, whether that is on a bank that owns up to 75% of our property, which is guaranteed by a government; on the continued love of our partners as it becomes a financial necessity; or on the generosity of our family members, or sadly sometimes on the generosity of their wills.

The pressure to be a property owner in the UK is inherited from the success of Baby Boomers, who have seen huge capital growth on their properties, benefiting from its affordability when they themselves were in their 20s. From their perspective, therefore, renting is madness and a waste of money. Their expectations are that their children should also be aiming to buy, rather than rent, adding further fuel to the fire of pressure that young people are up against. This desperate drive to save for up for property ownership puts added focus on salary, pushing thoughts of career happiness further and further away.

The family life that many of our parents took for granted, a reward for their hard work that they never needed to consciously think about, has been pushed further and further back into the futures of millennials. For many it is becoming a choice of career or children, with the added problem of women still facing a pay penalty for choosing the latter.[17] [18] [19]

The social contract has been broken.

The debate between generations is raging and, more often than not, it is confrontational and strewn with accusations.

There are, though, some hard truths to consider.

Despite this broken social contract, we demand more than any before us and many of our elders have been vocal in criticising us for that. We have been accused of being lazy, fickle and ungrateful. We want flexibility and fulfilment on top of a better salary, a home and, at some point, a family.

We want it all and we have been raised to fully expect it all.

How can we level such demands at a time when the average millennial must spend an unsustainable 57% of their salary on rent alone; how can we demand both career fulfilment and personal prosperity in this climate?[20] How can we be both the first generation to be worse off than their parents in adulthood whilst also be so demanding of change in the workplace?

Perhaps this is our way of rebelling against that broken social contract, as we are simply no longer willing to play the game of the rat race as the cost-benefit makes it simply not worth it. We have been let down, so why work as hard as our parents for a substantially smaller reward? Subconsciously, perhaps we are asking, 'what's the point?'

We are no longer willing to settle for the status quo.

There is one area that we can change though.

It is the only area that we are currently making headway with: our aim for fulfilment and flexibility from the workplace.

Perhaps what is perceived as the traits that make us whiny, self-entitled and demanding stem from our current lack of ability to better ourselves even if we do play the game and work hard. The lack of a social contract has raised fulfilment and flexibility to be our headline issues to make up for the lack of reward.

We have control over our own career happiness, and we should make sure that we seize it with both hands.

Interview with the expert: Corporate Solicitor to Homeless Supporter

I met Josh Taylor in an Afghan restaurant. We broke the ice over a 'couple's selection' of charcoal grilled meat, daal and some obligatory buttered naan. We share a passion for Central and South Asia, having met the year before in Kyrgyzstan.

Josh has made some interesting life choices, and so I sheepishly asked if I could interview him. I found his initial experiences and subsequent decisions immensely re-assuring, as I saw parallels with my own. I hope others, too, can draw inspiration and confidence from his happy ending.

Josh 2.0 – The Charity Worker

As a rough-sleeping prevention officer, Josh currently works for New Hope Trust, a North-London based charity. There, he spends his mornings preparing breakfasts and chatting to his service users, and in the afternoons, meets with them individually and visits areas where he knows they congregate. His passion for his job is obvious as his face lights up when I ask why he works there; he feels like he is 'doing something worthwhile every day' and can measure his achievements by literally changing the lives of those less fortunate. He loves building relationships with people and understanding what 'makes them tick'. As he continues, I realise that he is referring to mental health issues, rather than innocuous personality quirks.

I ask him to tell me about his first-hand experiences of why people find themselves in such horrendous situations. Josh becomes even more animated, telling me how so many of us assume that all homeless people are 'criminals, drunks, drug addicts and people with no future or real hope'. Of course, this is far from the truth.

'These people are just like everyone else, except they have been hit by unfortunate circumstances and have been through tragic situations that most of us will never experience, and don't have the support networks in place to get them through.'

He highlights the importance and seriousness of mental health as a major issue when people don't have family or close friends to fall back on. They are not vulnerable in an obvious way so slip through the net that society is supposed to provide.

He finds it difficult to compartmentalise the things he hears and sees in his work from his personal life, though he says it's worth it. Josh is also more than willing to accept the 50% pay cut from his old legal job. Why? Because the 'sense of fulfilment' he feels from his job and having a positive direction, in his and others' lives, 'more than compensates for it'.

Josh 1.0 – The Lawyer

Josh comes from a family of lawyers and relished 'debating and playing devil's advocate' growing up so much that he never questioned what seemed like the obvious career path. It is a well-paid and prestigious career, and so he skipped off after university to Law School.

It is easy to ignore that voice in the back of your head that initially goes off like a fire alarm when you feel that something is wrong.

But the more it is ignored, the quieter it can get. The voice can be placated and seduced into thinking it is mistaken. The weight of expectation, though often well intentioned and unspoken, is heavy and it is easy to be distracted by the highs and lows of life, especially when you are a young and enthusiastic student (enthusiastic for things other than your studies, in many cases).

Josh placated his inner voice by the thought that while he may not be the most conscientious law student, when it came to doing the actual job, he would enjoy it far more so the desire to work hard would naturally follow. After graduating, it seemed nonsensical to **not** try and become a fully qualified solicitor.

So, the next life stage followed and he won a place on a trainee scheme at a commercial solicitor's firm. It started with sleepless nights, and soon the voice was back and this time it could not be disregarded as easily. 'Within four months of starting I knew I would have to quit the minute I qualified,' which was then two years away. The realisation that the last five or six years would be a 'waste' though was difficult to bear. Slowly, the sleepless nights got worse and Josh began to explain how during that time he felt as though, professionally, his life was pointless.

As he went into more detail, we ignored the dessert menu now in front of us.

Despite muddling on through, he describes this time as 'hellish' and outlines how he became a 'different person, far less sociable and confident, always thinking about and dreading work'. Josh described how a lack of confidence could affect every part of your life, how you become resigned to your situation but still live in a constant state of panic.

What he is depicting is something I am familiar with, the knowledge that you are desperately unhappy on a daily basis but not knowing how to take control of that. It's like he had watched my experience and was repeating it back to me. The knowledge that I was not alone was more comforting than any sympathetic shoulder had been during that time.

Then he said it – 'I was depressed'. Perhaps not clinically diagnosed, but it certainly sounded damaging. Josh's body language had changed; the impact clearly had a physical effect too.

But then came the golden moment – 'on the day I qualified, I stuck to my word and quit.' Josh then spent three months travelling through Japan, South Korea, the Philippines, China and finally Central Asia, where I had met him. Afterwards, he decided to move back in with his parents and spent six months volunteering for a range of ex-offender charities in Manchester, eventually getting his job as a rough-sleeping prevention officer.

As we're leaving, Josh tells me that he thinks life is about enjoyment. He advises me that I choose something for the experience and enjoyment, not the salary.

One thing that had certainly become clear over the evening was that it is our social relationships with friends and family that are important, far more so than material possessions – all too easily the lack of the former could to lead to the lack of the latter, not the other way around.

Points for consideration

- *That* Sunday night feeling can be a good one.

- Life isn't always about doing what is rational.

- You are not alone in having a quarter life career crisis.

- Being miserable in your job shouldn't be the norm, and for too many of us it is.

- If you have felt 'meh' about your job, avoid the subject when someone asks about your day, or when cornered you say that 'it's not that bad, it's just a job' – it doesn't have to be that way.

- When they are young, each generation has it 'the hardest it's ever been'.

- The Game of Life is shit.

- Being just OK shouldn't be OK.

- Millennials have gone from being the most privileged generation growing up to the least privileged in adulthood, leading to the frustration of a prolonged adolescence for many of us.

- The yawning gap between the high expectations we have been raised to have on entering the workforce and trying to enter the property market, and the stark difference of the reality is the source of many of our problems.

- The social contract has been broken.

- Fulfilment and flexibility at work is the only issue millennials can influence about their futures at the moment.

Questions to reflect on

- Can you separate a bad day from a bad job?

- What makes you happy; are you happy now?

- Has your behaviour changed? Could this be due to you being unhappy at work?

CHAPTER TWO

ON WHAT TO DO NEXT

on having ideas:
if at first the idea is not absurd, then there is no hope for it.
– albert einstein

on implementing them:
everything you possess of skill, and wealth, and handicraft, wasn't it first merely a thought and a quest?
– rumi

On touching back down in the UK following my summer holiday, I had to consider exactly how I was going to seize my own career happiness. I had to face up to the question of 'what's next?'.

When I stood outside my office on Monday morning, imagining that I was somewhere else, I assumed a specific job would come to mind, or at least a general career area, or just some direction at all. I drew a blank – a total mental blank. The longer I stood there, the less I could imagine what sorts of ideas I should be having. It should be obvious, shouldn't it? I should innately know what I wanted. Except, I didn't. I felt like I was at one of life's key decision points and there was a fork in my road but one of the paths was completely obscured from view.

I could carry on trying to find a job in the areas that I had been aiming for within the public sector and which my degrees had prepared me for. It made sense, I had an education and now some good experience that I could build on. If I went down that road, everyone would understand why I was leaving, including my future employers. So why wasn't I leaping head first into it? Why wasn't I channelling all my enthusiasm for hating my current job into finding a new one?

For once, I didn't instinctively want to do the sensible thing. For once, I wanted to do something that seemed entirely nonsensical. The old 'good girl' Emma that followed the rules was morphing into someone new, someone different. I wanted to try other things, things I had always wondered about but had never seriously considered. Things that I didn't really believe I could do, things that I wasn't sure were even real jobs.

Indecision continued a little while longer though. Pursuing the sensible path seemed like the right thing to do. But yet I couldn't quite bring myself to follow it. I wanted to rebel. To break free of what had become a monotonous life and just do things differently. I wanted to do things my way for once. I wanted to have my own opinions, for those to be taken seriously and for them to matter. I wanted to express myself differently to how I had been taught to express myself. I strongly felt the old idiom of a 'square peg in a round hole', a hole I'd been trying to convince myself that I fit into for my entire conscious life.

I hadn't given career advice a thought since I was 17, and even then I hadn't given it much consideration, just always doing what I knew would enable me to enter the next stage in the game. Now, I was stumped. All my hard work throughout education and employment had led to nothing, so why would the next career path I tried be any different?

Career education while growing up was concentrated around taking multiple choice tests about your personality that then spat out your top few best career matches. It was akin to taking a Facebook quiz to tell you which Mean Girls character you were most like according to your star sign. In my school's careers quiz, I got Dental Nurse. I honestly cannot think of a more unsuitable career – my only irrational phobia is of dentists.

Obviously much more thought went into those personality tests than MeanGirl87 put into theirs, but the meaning of the results was fairly similar, as was how seriously I took the respective outcomes. Just before choosing my A-Levels in Year 11, we had one-on-one sessions with a professional careers councillor. I was 15 at the time and was totally clueless about what any job really entailed, and even more clueless on what I wanted to do for a living. The kindly, elderly councillor gave me a copy of a careers directory book that covered 92 different career types and sent me off to read it. That was pretty much it for careers education. Those who are unsure of their career aspirations are one of the least likely to receive careers guidance.[21]

Sifting through the pages, it was fascinating to see all the different options out there, laid out in full, one after another, for the first time. Looking back at the dusty book today, I can see that I had earmarked eight careers to look into further, all those years ago. Not one of them am I remotely interested in pursuing as an adult. Now, I would earmark nine totally separate careers that I have formerly worked in, am working in now or would be interested in working in at some point in my life (most of the 25 of the careers I have actually tried were listed). 15-year-old me clearly didn't give those ones a second thought. What we think we want as teenagers is often vastly different to what we decide we want in other life stages, in our 20s, 30s, 40s and beyond.

The issue with careers education in this form is its one dimensionality. Career options are presented as a finite and linear list without any implication that you can do more than one of them or that there was any crossover between them. As a teenager, I simply did not know that scientific publishing could exist, I had never heard of the psychology of economics, the mathematics of music, or of archaeologist working with construction engineers. The notion of career change didn't exist while growing up either, even if as adults we now know differently. At the time, your career choice was implicitly presented as something that you would follow through with until you retired – that was that. There was, therefore, an immense pressure to choose the 'right' GCSEs that would pave the way for you to choose the 'right' A-Levels (or BTECs, NVQs…), which in turn allowed you to study the 'right' university course, letting you finally apply for the 'right' job. It all felt so pre-determined.

There was simply no room for just trying out all of those eight careers I had earmarked. You could try one, certainly, through the prescribed week of work experience in Year 10. You could maybe stretch it to two careers if you had been an especially astute and self-motivated teenager. At that age though, most of us were more interested in who had kissed who at a party last weekend, or if you could hide your tipsiness from your parents when they picked you up from a party the following weekend. It's not that we didn't care about our futures, many of us cared deeply; it's more that life didn't feel like it could really exist beyond the end of school or college, it felt so distant as to be abstract and incomprehensible. Like many of our classmates, we just got on with the ups and downs of teenage life, assuming that somewhere along the way it would all work itself out as long as we followed the path, played the game and did our best.

The idea that we could actually go and try out all the different careers we were interested in before committing to one didn't exist. The importance placed on work experience and time put aside to it was negligible. It was a means to an end, another box to tick, another game to play. Concepts such as the gig economy, portfolio careers and the coming impact of automation on different sectors certainly didn't exist either, along with emerging industries like cyber security or skills like coding becoming mainstream. In fairness, some of these would have been difficult to predict a decade ago and even harder to make their importance heard to a group of teenagers. Passing next lesson's mock chemistry exam was a far more pressing matter.

Later on, when it came to internships, you had to fight to prove your absolute commitment to wanting a career in that industry. Placements were often as competitive as actual jobs. You had to say that it had been your life-long goal since childhood and demonstrate your longstanding interest by talking about the work experience you had already done, the articles you had read and talks that you had attended to prove your point. Many of us sincerely did all of that and meant every word we said. But, the point is that we were never really trying it on for size, we had already had to commit ourselves to it to even have the opportunity to try it out. There was no real space to just give it a go and see what we thought. If you admitted you didn't like it, you would have to start proving your life-long dedication to another career path all over again.

What we need is the ability to try out as many of our career interests as possible without the need to prove it being our heartfelt desire from early childhood. Young people need time, whether that is in school holidays or in the summer term after exams, to gain work experience in multiple careers over several years, while stressing the importance of reflecting on and understanding what they do and do not like about each one. Careers education should not be an added extra. There are slow rumblings of change for pupils today, with the publication of a Careers Strategy by the Department for Education in December 2017.[22] However, until learning by doing through a programme of work experience in a diverse range of careers is accessible to all students, the impact is questionable.

But what about you, now, as someone who has long-finished with the education system but is still just as unsure as you were then?

At the time, I had all these contradictory thoughts swirling around in my mind and my inner narrative was making less and less sense. Pushing back against everything I knew in terms of how the world of work actually works was terrifying, it left a gaping hole with one burning question, to which I had no answers: 'If I wasn't going to leave my job for another one, then what was I going to do?'

Clarity came during yet another evening spent stewing on the couch. I had no ideas to fall back on, no ideas except for careers that were silly childhood fantasies.

And there lay the answer. I considered the question: 'What if I could do all my childhood dream jobs? Every single one of them.'

It was in not knowing that I found some direction.

I decided to write a list of all the different careers I had ever wanted to try; from the point where you are asked as a child what you want to be when you grow up and you would say astronaut, firefighter, train driver, chef, or prime minister.

So, I started writing a list and without really intending to, I ended up with a list of 22 different careers. These were 22 different jobs that I had harboured some secret curiosity, longing or fascination for. If I could do anything in the world, if there were no obstacles or barriers, then maybe I would like to do one of those. I also had three question marks. I left some space at the bottom of the page for careers that I didn't know of yet, things that I didn't even know that I might like to do. That gave me 25.

On my list were some traditional, sensible careers that I felt I should still consider. There were also obscure and almost random ideas, half-formed that had been lying dormant for years. There were things that not even I was taking seriously when I wrote them down. Plenty of them seemed like they weren't 'real' jobs, but they were still things that someone, somewhere did for a living. Now might finally be the time for me to see if I could be one of those people.

I laid back on the sofa and started day-dreaming, picturing Emma The Explorer, Emma The Archaeologist, Emma The Author. There was Emma The Big-Shot TV Producer, then there was Emma The Hard-Nosed Investigative Reporter. Emma The Crime-Busting Police Officer also featured, along with Emma The Super-Cool Tech Start-up Founder.

There were so many different possible selves to choose from. So many of them seemed both unobtainable and just within reach at the same time. I tried to picture my life in all these new, exciting scenarios. Each one was totally unidentifiable from my current reality. Very few of them involved routine and predictability. Office work featured in some of them, but few were entirely office-based. Was I just looking for a life that was different to my present and it didn't really matter in what way it was different? Change for the sake of needing change? Or was it deeper than that – were there specific kinds of change that I wanted and, perhaps, needed? How do you even begin to unpick that?

I started to think about what exactly it was about my current job and working life that I hated so much, realising that perhaps I needed to identify specific things to make sure I didn't find myself back in the same situation. Being sat at a desk was certainly one thing, as was a long commute. The routine of life too I found deeply problematic. Of course, all life needs some structure and repetition, but what if I could find something with at least some greater variety? It occurred to me that these were very environmental problems, and weren't really about the work itself, though still felt just as important as they were a significant contribution to my misery at work.

With the actual work, part of the problem centred around the fact that I didn't feel like I mattered, that I could have not gone into work for a month and things would have kept ticking on just the same. It wasn't that I was necessarily bad at what I did, or that I wouldn't be missed as a person, more that my job itself wouldn't be. Basically, I felt like I'd had bullshit jobs, and I wanted to feel like I was personally adding some value in whatever I was doing. Then there was the making a difference thing, the reason I had gone down the public sector path in the first place, I wanted that again to give me a sense of purpose.

What is it, exactly, that you hate about your job?

Identify and write down all the different things you don't like about your current job, or even your career. Think through both the actual work you do and your working environment, as well as trying to recognise if any of it is related to the individuals you work with – 44% of people leave their job because of a bad boss.

Try to do this exercise twice; on a good and separately on a bad day, before comparing your responses on a third day. This will give you a fairer and more objective overview.

Do you need to change job or change career?

Are the things that you have listed previously issues with your job specifically or are they things that would be problems that are endemic to your career more widely? Separately, from the previous question, put each point under one of two columns – a 'job' column or 'career' column. This will give you a clearer idea of where the problem lies. For example, a lack of office camaraderie would be specific to the job and fall under the 'job' column. On the other hand, competitiveness could be specific to the career itself, consequently it would fall under the 'career' column.

Be honest about this – try to identify which issues belong where.

All your issues could end up in the job column and you still want to change career anyway. That's totally fine. You could just want a change of career and just don't know what to do next. It's perfectly OK to not feel the need to justify it and work it all out in detail. If you do feel this way, still try to give this exercise a go, as it will be helpful when we later come to identify the things we **are** looking for in a career.

As the days passed, I couldn't get the idea of multiple different possible 'selves' out of my head. How could I possibly choose one without trying it first? But how would I know which one to pick without having anything other than a job I hated to compare it to? By that comparison, I had fallen in love with the first alternative I tried and would stop there.

Does it matter then which one I choose, I asked myself? If I got sucked back in to playing life's game then the answer would be no, it does not matter, as long as it's marginally better than your present. But this just didn't sit right – again, intuition stuck its nosy self in what should have been a closing door.

It **does** matter which path you choose, which 'self' you want as your own.

All the different options and possibilities of choice were overwhelming; especially because of how many of my views were based on glamorised ideals of what it must be like to be an interior designer or an investigative journalist.

I knew it was easy to romanticise career paths – the Graduate Scheme I was on is one of the more competitive out there, with a great marketing team. I was often contacted by students, recent graduates and professionals up to their early 30s who wanted in. The public sector might not objectively sound like a 'sexy' career choice, but for ambitious young professionals who wanted the challenge and status of working somewhere where less than 4% of applicants are accepted, it really is. Many were there because they sincerely wanted to make a difference, but a secondary unspoken reason was the exclusivity – wanting to prove that you are better than the 96%. The desirability of the career I'd chosen had compounded the guilt I had felt in wanting to leave it, but it had also demonstrated that just because it's a competitive career path, doesn't mean that it's necessarily right for me.

What I was slowly realising was that I wanted to try out all the different versions of myself. This was mostly driven by a deep-rooted need to know what living those lives might actually be like, rather than guessing, assuming and idealising. It was also partly driven by fear; the thought of not really knowing what I was getting myself into for my next career move and then ending up in the same situation, or even worse than where I currently was, made me feel nauseous with anxiety. From the frying pan into the fire, as they say.

I was soon to turn 24. What if I set myself the goal of trying all 25 before my 25th birthday?

Yes, I wanted to try them. All.

25 CAREERS

ARCHAEOLOGY

TRAVEL
WRITING

PHOTOGRAPHY

PUBLISHING

PROPERTY
DEVELOPMENT

FARMING

INVESTIGATIVE
JOURNALISM

NEWS
REPORTER

CHARITY

CRISIS
MANAGEMENT

MOVIE EXTRA

INTERNATIONAL
SECURITY

FOREST SCHOOL
TEACHER

TOUR GUIDE

CREATIVE
MARKETING

THINK TANK

GARDEN
DESIGNER

TV PRODUCTION

COUNTER-TERRORISM
POLICE UNIT

INTERIOR
DESIGN

TECH STARTUP

POLICE - DOG
UNIT

EXPLORER

BLOGGER

AUTHOR

One of the good things I have found about the feeling of having nothing to lose is that it makes you far more open-minded to the odd crazy idea. That meant that I didn't immediately dismiss the thought as a ridiculous, immature hare-brained scheme as I would have ordinarily done. This time the idea continued to bubble around inside my head, excitingly and enticingly. I kept trying to forget about it, to put it to one side, but it wouldn't disappear. It would creep up on me on the train to work, catch me when I would pause outside the office and surprise me when I was illicitly browsing job boards.

I wanted the opportunity to try things out for a month, a week, or even just a day, to see if there really were things that I had ruled out on the bumpy path to disillusioned adulthood, when perhaps I shouldn't have. I was desperate to double-check and wanted to see if I would make a good teacher, farmer or photographer. What about the times I had secretly dreamed of being a luxury property developer, tour guide or landscape gardener? Finally, there were the jobs that I had always held a secret longing for but seemed to be such unrealistic aspirations – blue-sky thinking – like being an author.

If I followed through with this idea, would I ever be employed again afterwards? It would either make me the most or the least employable person, and I had no idea of the way it might actually go. How would I be able to afford to pay rent, eat, or just live for that matter? 25 jobs in a year is roughly one every two weeks, was that long enough? Could I organise all of this? Would 25 companies even agree to take me on?

Leaving your job to work in another is one thing, even leaving your job with the intention of applying for others is just about acceptable, but that level of indecision on a career would make me look fickle, volatile even. Future employers might think that I would never be loyal to them, that I would never be able to hold down a job for long enough to be worth employing. I could be classed as a generalist who was so general that I couldn't have any sincere depth of knowledge on anything at all.

On the flip side, if I could carry the whole thing off, maybe it would show real initiative, creativity and integrity, as well as a sincere commitment to professional development. It might show a future employer that I could solve problems, could very quickly learn new skills and was willing to put my money where my mouth was. Perhaps it would demonstrate an ability to ask difficult questions and challenge norms, seeing wider trends across industries, helping to avoid the dangers of groupthink.

I saw how this could be divisive though, and dependent on the type of person a future boss was. Ever the optimist, I went with the latter.

To get another perspective on this, I arranged to meet with a senior and successful former boss whose opinion I really respected to ask her views. Over a cup of tea, I pitched my ideas to her and I could see her polite smile turn to a frown, and then turn to a grimace. She didn't get it. She didn't understand at all. She thought it sounded like career suicide. I might just get away with it because of my youth, it might get put down as a form of gap year or an early sabbatical to broaden my skills. But that would just be the excuse, the lame justification for a year out of permanent employment. It could be an embarrassing gap in my CV.

I left the meeting disheartened. She had thrown up some very fair challenges that were similar to the ones I had already been mulling over. That was why I had chosen to ask her of all people, after all. I would have to consider my explanations and responses to them if I was going to go for it.

In thinking through my motivation at least, I considered how important it was to know oneself, to really understand who I am and what I wanted. I had not given it any real thought before. I didn't really know what I liked and what I didn't, instead I had spent my time drifting from one step of the game to the next. But then, how was I meant to know if I had never really tried anything else before? It was like the career version of marrying my very first boyfriend. Gag.

Careers should be like dating; very few of us marry the person we first meet, so why do we tend to pursue the very first career we try? On average, we have seven to eight relationships before finding 'the one', but with our careers we tend to go with a single decision we make in our teens or, at most, early 20s.[23] In our dating lives, we try out plenty of different people, with countless first dates, on average 15 first kisses and five one-night stands.[24] Given that we spend at least as much time at work as we do with our partners, we think vastly more about trying out our options in our personal lives than we do in our professional. We invest plenty more in it too; consider the cost of all the meals, drinks and transport, as well as the huge time investment too. The average single Brit spends £1280 per year on dating, and that's before you factor in the costs you will have when in an actual relationship.[25]

How much time and money did you put towards considering your career decision, flirting with different career ideas and options? You have bought and are currently reading this book, along with maybe a few others. Your workplace might have sent you on a training course or two, but they probably footed the bill and you may not have had a choice in it. A few years ago, you may well have worked unpaid as an intern, paying with the opportunity cost, lunches and train fares or petrol. Overall though, it is likely far from £1280 a year.

You could make the same case for your taste in literature, film or food even. If you had only ever eaten one cuisine or seen one genre of film, how would you ever know what the other possibilities were? You would never know what you were missing. Imagine the first time you read a *Harry Potter* book, that first film that made you see the world through someone else's eyes, the first time you discovered a pizzeria that makes the best stone-baked pepperoni pizzas this side of Naples; can you imagine life without those experiences now?

I wanted that for my career, for it to enrich life rather than detract from it – I was convinced that I would find a way to make it work.

If I could come out of this project having found what I really wanted to do, with the perfect job, colleagues and a boss I liked, what would that mean? I'd be a happy employee. If you are a happy employee, you are likely to take fewer sick days – both for your physical and mental health, and you will be more motivated, engaged and efficient.[26] This view is a popular one, with on-going studies since the 1920s on the 'happy-productive worker hypothesis'.[27][28] Economists argue that there is a positive correlation between when an employee is happy in their surroundings and has good relationships with colleagues, for example, with their productivity.[29] These two contributing factors have as much effect on performance as someone's innate ability to do the job.

If we look at this from a purely business perspective, happy employees will work harder, and feel a greater sense of loyalty to their employer. Happy employees will not only get the job done quicker, but will also improve staff retention rates, reducing recruitment and initial training costs. There is a 3% increase in revenue for 5% increase in employee engagement.[30] Being happy in your workplace is good for business, dramatically so.[31][32]

Now scale that up. Look beyond the individual perspective, beyond the company, even beyond the industry or sector, to a national overview. Work happiness could actively strengthen an economy.[33] The increased productivity could lead to a higher GDP.[34] Happier employees mean healthier employees, too.[35][36][37][38] This could start to help reduce pressure on already stretched resources, including physical and mental healthcare services.

More solid and practical justifications on the logistics were needed though. If I was really going to do this then it needed to be more than just aimlessly following a few friends of friends around for a year. At first, I considered it at the personal level; exposure to so many different careers in a short space of time meant that, by the end, I would really know what I wanted to do. Wherever I ended up afterwards, I would be there with my whole heart and would be conscientious and loyal for the rest of my working life. I would want to get up every Monday morning. That mattered for me, but it would also make me a more productive worker.

I would also be able to learn a huge amount from observing how so many industries worked; maybe it would mean I would see things differently and be able to offer a unique perspective on problems. I would gain insight into the best (and worst!) practices in different industries and be able to apply those lessons and observations, warning against others, wherever I ended up. Then there were all the new skills I could learn from the placements I would do. I would get very good at quickly building rapport and developing relationships with all the new people I would constantly be meeting. My teamwork and communication skills more generally would rocket. Maybe I could start sharing what I would learn on social media and through a blog. I could write about the issues of career happiness and fulfilment more widely and about the problems that the millennial generation faces in the workplace. The digital and written communication skills would definitely be useful wherever I ended up and learning about website design and marketing could hardly be a bad thing – I might even discover a love for them. That was more than enough to talk myself into it.

My finances needed much more thought though. I had managed to build up some savings from working since graduating that I could rely on if I lived very frugally for a little while. My social life would shrink, I was going to limit going out for drinks or a meal as much as I possibly could. I wouldn't buy any new clothes. I would also try to do bits of freelance and part-time work over the year to help earn some cash to cover my costs. I hoped placements would at least cover my expenses, if not an actual salary. The biggest cost was obviously rent. I was very lucky that I was able to move back home with my parents, just like one of 3.4 million other millennials who live at home.[39][40] It would have to be enough; as long as I could cover my costs without going over my overdraft limit, it should be just about do-able. I tried to think about the project as an investment in my future happiness and career; if I was going to be working until I was 70, then not earning £20k for a year probably wouldn't make all that much difference in the long run.

This is where the philosophy of living life with no regrets came in; you are presented with a choice. When you are in your 80s, which path or decision will you look back on and remember with pride and pleasure? Which one will make the greatest positive change in your life, or the lives of others? These questions consciously guided my decision-making process. Within reason, I've always found this mental trick invaluable in helping to see a future path more clearly. It may sound almost condescendingly simple, but when you put a life decision in that context, it is an incredibly useful tool to see through the murk.

I considered the worst-case scenario; I couldn't arrange any other placements, or I ran out of money. Basically, what if I failed spectacularly? Aside from the public embarrassment (social media generally has a short memory), I had put my tail between my legs and started hunting for another job in earnest, focusing on a better paid private sector ones to try and make up the money. The savings could provide just enough of a buffer until I got back on my feet in a month or two. The best-case scenario was that I would succeed at the project and end up with my dream job, or jobs, at the end of the year.

We are in such a rush when we are young to get on with life. Time seems to simultaneously be at its slowest and its fastest; we blink and a month or four have zipped past without us even noticing. At the same time, we can count every single minute of every single interminable working day. Our working life, though, will be long – very long. Those of us born in the 1980s and 1990s should expect to work throughout to age 70 and quite possibly beyond.[41] As both life expectancy and the quality of life for older people improves, we will be both physically and mentally able to work for longer, as well as quite possibly needing to work for longer to meet the financial requirements of an aging population.

There are plenty of implications of this for career happiness and fulfilment, as we are more likely than any generation before us to have multiple career changes. We will want different things at different times in our lives and have different requirements and obligations – that is something that we need to embrace.

At this stage of the journey, though, the solace was more in knowing that in the grand scheme of life, taking a year out at 24 to focus on figuring out what you might like to do for the rest of your career is not going to ruin your life. In the long-term, it's more likely to have a positive impact than a negative one as you will come away with a far better understanding of yourself and what you want. It would vastly improve mental health and wellbeing. All of this can be argued to be far more beneficial than an additional year's experience and salary in a role that you hate and never want to do again.

All of this stacked up to become enough good reasons to take the plunge. It made what outwardly sounded a very risky decision seem less risky. It made it seem like it might be worthwhile.

If you could try out any careers, which ones would you choose?

Create a list of all the different career ideas you have ever wondered about, that have been sitting in the back of your mind for months, years, decades even, and the ones that only occur to you when you start writing. They don't have to be 'real' jobs, they can be jobs which you think might not even exist. They might be jobs or even causes you would like to dedicate yourself to wholly, or they could be things which you kind of like the idea of for one day or even afternoon per week.

Leave some space at the end for ideas you haven't thought of yet. Start talking to friends and family for ideas, ask what their dream job would be.

Having some ideas for a direction, however tenuous and incomplete, helped. It helped to temporarily dull that feeling of urgency to leave. That feeling was still there, but I now had something to aim for, something that I was going to work towards and it was enough to get me through each day more comfortably. I could wait for another few weeks without feeling like I was losing my mind and focus on developing my ideas instead; it's all about the small steps.

I started building a website; I felt like I needed a place to record everything that was running through my head, a 21st century open diary. It was more than that though, I needed to visualise what the whole thing might look like before taking the next step. The process of creating something that I knew could be seen by others helped to focus my thinking, allowing me to develop ideas in more detail and start planning things out a little more in advance.

Website design is something I knew absolutely nothing about prior to deciding that I wanted to do it, except for copy and pasting html codes into MySpace, aged 12. This seemed like a very good way to start the year of trying new things. Two weeks and three or four terrible designs in, I finally managed to create the first version of my website. The hosting and domain name came in at about £60 per year, which, given that I hadn't quite yet handed in my notice, didn't break the bank.

It was all the tiny details which took the most time, things like logos, colour schemes and images, making sure your pages don't take five minutes to load, and ensuring the whole thing works well across different operating systems and on mobile phones too. After I'd gotten all of that nailed, there was the question of 'how does anyone find my website?' to answer. I had to get to grips with the basics of Search Engine Optimisation (SEO), I had no idea beforehand that you have to actually physically list a website on Google, I had just assumed that was an automatic thing. Turns out no. After I'd figured that out, I then needed the website to be listed high enough in Google's listings that someone is likely to click on it. When was the last time you looked at a website on page 17?

After thinking about someone miraculously coming across my website is on a search engine, social media was the most obvious way to get word out. That felt more intimidating though, as it meant that anything I wrote could be read by people I actually knew. Despite feeling nervous, I knew that telling others what I was doing more openly would be a way of holding myself to account. All of this took six weeks' work in evenings and on weekends.

The next step was writing something down. I wanted to explain why I was going to resign, partly to others and partly to myself – it wasn't all quite as logically coherent as it is with the benefit of hindsight.

I wrote and re-wrote. I talked about valuing a work/life balance, wanting a fulfilling career and how I felt unable to move past the mundane routine of inactivity that daily life had become. I questioned if there was another way of doing things – a question that I'm still trying to answer now to help the others that lie awake at night wondering if they could choose a different path.

At this point, I decided I better get going to organise some of the first placements – I wanted the security of having the first few organised before I actually left work, almost as a proof of concept.

Archaeology was first on the list, something I
had wanted to try since watching Indiana Jones as
a child. I had taken a few modules in the subject at
university but had worried that it wasn't a 'real' job
so, despite loving it, had left studying it behind.
Nevertheless, I called up my old archaeology
professor, explained my ideas for the sabbatical
and asked if he might know of any excavations
that I could take part in over the next few months.
Whilst I'm certain that he didn't quite remember
who I was, he rather surprisingly said yes. The university was helping
to run an excavation of a Roman site in Transylvania, Romania, in two
weeks' time and would be understaffed, could I join the team and help?

What?!

Slightly overcome by the bizarre randomness, I stuttered, and then
recovered with an overly enthusiastic 'yes'. It was the first step towards
making this slightly absurd plan of mine actually happen – I was
committing to starting, not just talking about it anymore.

I had two weeks left of annual leave in my job that I had not been
planning to use. A quick conversation with my boss to approve the
time off, and that was it. I was going to Transylvania to see what being
an archaeologist in the field was like.*

Following my experience as an archaeologist I returned to the UK,
browned from the Romanian sun, and I started looking around for my
next couple of placements. I decided that if I could get these secured,
then I could quit with some confidence.

The next career I had my eye on was being a farmer. It was
certainly idealised in my mind – I loved the idea of working so closely
with animals and of being out in the countryside every day. The only
problem was that I couldn't think of anyone I could ask about it.

---

* Please refer to the end of each chapter to read about specific jobs.

To try and change this, I started asking friends and family if they knew of anyone. As word got around, a friend's mother got in touch to say that she had a friend who was now a farmer and would be happy to talk to me. And hopefully, my next placement.

I had decided while designing the website that I wanted to interview experts within the industries I would be trying out. Spending two weeks work shadowing in each job was hardly enough time to get anything more than relatively superficial insight into what it was actually like. It made sense, therefore, to go straight to those who had made each career their professional home and to ask them about the highs and lows of life. I wanted to ensure that I did not mistakenly glamorise a career path again, or was aware at least of when I was doing and so would try to challenge it, as I was with farming.

Interview with the expert: Farmer

Debbie Kingsley sounds like a woman you wouldn't want to mess with. She is an art consultant, a trainer, freelance writer, blogger, businesswoman and several other things in between. She is also a proud farmer.

'Complete serendipity' is how Debbie found herself in this career. Nice girls from North London do not usually end up with livestock and 100 acres in Devon. She is clearly someone who enjoys challenging the norm, with 'no time for makeup' or other vanities, up early working with her husband, Andrew, seven days a week.

Being a farmer is certainly not choosing life's easy path, and she repeatedly reminds me not to idealise the lifestyle – it is hard work and will mean spending much of your time cold, wet and tired. When we speak at 10am, she has already taken a steer (castrated male) to the abattoir, fed all the animals, done the mucking out, checked the cattle and sheep, and taken the dogs for a walk. That's just the pre-breakfast routine. Meanwhile, I had settled down to a cup of tea before drawing up some questions for our interview. If I want to be a farmer, I need to say goodbye to my treasured weekend lie-ins.

As we continue speaking, her passion for her career choice and lifestyle shines through, and she tells me how being outdoors on a sunny day surrounded by green fields and healthy animals never gets old, even after nearly three decades. She seems to genuinely love getting up in the morning to do her job, something so many of us dream of.

Of course, the days it rains are a little more difficult. But Debbie tells me that once she's up it's fine and, if anything, the worse the weather, 'the more care the animals need.'

This is a point I had not considered, and I can see how it would spur you up even on the bleakest of mornings.

South Yeo Farm West focuses on rare and native breeds, with over 100 ewes, cattle, pigs and poultry. This is because Debbie and Andrew share a philosophy of supporting native breeds to increase the diversity of gene pools, and besides this, local breeds will do best on the land they were selectively bred for over the course of generations. Of course, this is a business, she reminds me, so all are also chosen for their great tasting meat. The farm sends meat boxes directly to clients rather than to supermarkets, as it means they earn more per animal, which is crucial for a small business wanting to remain in control and maximise profits. Supplying supermarkets means farmers are reliant on the prices set in head offices, which are much more likely to vary. Her enthusiasm for this business model is evident, and she clearly takes pride in rearing an animal through its lifecycle, to be able to supply a very high-quality product to her loyal customer base.

This is a stark reminder that, of course, killing animals is part of the business and we spend a while discussing this point. She sympathises and sincerely finds it sad, but 'it is the circle of life' and she is proud to give each animal the best quality of life she can. Ultimately though, it is how she makes a living. This is an issue that it could be easy to get emotional about, especially given that many of us are now so removed from where our food originates. Whilst I am not sentimental about it, I do feel very strongly about the quality of life of animals reared for their meat, milk, eggs and wool. However, as Debbie highlights, this is part of the job, and my concerns can be minimised as I would be the one in control.

She then begins to tell me that she believes farmers are massively underestimated and makes a convincing argument.

They need to be the vet, midwife, entrepreneur, marketer, distributer, negotiator, and an astute businessperson, as well as being a general DIY god, make hay and a whole host of other things. Let's not forget her other work as an art consultant, a freelance writer, a trainer and so on. It becomes apparent that to be successful in this career you need to be very organised, self-motivated and good at time management, as on a smaller farm you need several strands of income. Fortunately, I am a big fan of portfolio careers, so this would suit me just fine.

My interviewee was far too busy to let me follow her around for a couple of weeks, telling me in no uncertain terms that I would be more of a hindrance than a help for such a short period of time. Fair enough! What she did offer to do instead, though, was to send a tweet out to her 5,000 followers to ask if any of them might be able to help.

Within ten minutes, I had a farmer asking if I could come and work with her. I loved that I had accidentally managed to find not one, but two women farmers, which immediately served to break down any gender stereotypes around this career path. Enthusiastically, I arranged a call with Emma Collison, proud owner of Moor View Alpacas. Yes, you read that correctly, she ran an alpaca farm.

I gingerly rang her later that day, having no idea what to expect at the other end of the phone. A small part of me was concerned that she would be a psychopath, purely because she had agreed to this arrangement via social media. I needn't have worried. Emma was just as delighted as I was at the opportunity. She explained how she was always in need of help on her farm in Cornwall, and in exchange she was happy to give me room and board in her home for free. I leapt at her offer and asked when I could start. It was nearing the end of the summer and I wanted to make sure that I was able to visit her while there might still be a few bluebird days. There was a chuckle and the other end of the phone.

'Oh no. You can come in January, because if you enjoy farming in January, then you'll know that you are *meant* to be a farmer.'

It was the sort of logic that I couldn't rebut. She was quite right. If I could love farming on the days that offered only the worst of mid-winter British weather, then I would have found my calling. I slightly begrudgingly agreed to January.

Once that thorny issue was settled, I probed her on her animals. There really were plenty of alpacas, along with the more traditional sheep and a handful of pigs. There was even a farm cat.

Another part of why Emma wanted me there in January was that it would be the early lambing season and an extra pair of hands was always going to be useful. This reason I was far less reluctant about. Lambs – yes, I definitely wanted to help out with that!

The second placement was all booked in.

Next up, I looked at photography. There was only one person I knew of at the time who worked as a professional photographer, a woman I'd met on an internship that had nothing to do with photography several years ago. From a little social media stalking, I learned she was still snapping away and was working as a wedding photographer in Ibiza. This was another job that oozed glamour in my mind, especially on a Mediterranean island.

Feeling a little awkward as we hadn't spoken in years, I sent her a Facebook message explaining the project and asking if she might be interested. She replied instantly and said yes! She offered to put me up in her flat by the sea, I'd just need to get a cheap flight over, which was cheaper than a weekly train pass into London, and contribute for some food. We agreed a week where she had a wedding that would need a second photographer and I booked my plane ticket for a month's time.

Third placement, sorted.

Fourth on my list was publishing. The same internship where I met my now-photographer friend, I knew there was another woman who had since joined a guidebook publisher specialising in remote and adventurous travel, Bradt Guides. Another awkward Facebook message and another surprisingly easy yes – my fourth placement was lined up for straight after photography in Ibiza.

I took more of a gamble for the fifth placement. London Lofts are a property development start up that I had been admiring from afar for over a year. Every time I looked for my dream London penthouse flat or arty loft for when I might have a much higher income, their website is where I ended up. On a whim, I emailed their CEO and asked if

I could join them for a couple of weeks. Remarkably, I got a very enthusiastic yes back in a couple of hours.

In the space of a few days, I had four placements lined up, on top of the one I had already completed. A fifth of my experiences were now sorted before I'd even handed in my notice. Whilst I knew that they wouldn't all be so easy, I was shocked at how quickly they had been set up. It was enough reassurance, though, to give me the courage to follow through with my convictions and finally, formally hand in my notice.

Having only entered the world of work relatively recently, I didn't really know how to leave it. I started trying to draft a resignation letter, but kept faltering, knowing my absolute honesty might not be totally appreciated, understandably. I decided on organising a meeting with my boss and to worry about writing it all down later.

I had been getting increasingly anxious in the days leading up to our meeting, as I knew that once I had resigned there really was no turning back. Up until that point, everything was reversible with only some loss of face. No one at work would have been any wiser and I could have carried on with my job as if it hadn't happened. Getting five placements in careers that I'd always been curious about within the space of a few days, however, was the final push to follow through.

Watching a person's facial expression when you tell them that you are leaving a stable job for an absurd, self-concocted scheme is something I had to get used to. Bewilderment comes first; it takes a few moments to process something that initially sounds so utterly foolhardy. Initially, most are too focused on that to try to use a polite, if surprised, neutral tone of voice or eyebrow height. Then it goes one of two ways; there is either a scowl of judgement or a revelatory flash, after which comes a barrage of questions. Fortunately, my boss's face reflected the latter when we met later that week, as I explained why I was leaving.

The conversation went far better than I had dared imagine and ended with my giving them the link to my website, so they could follow my progress. Having my boss' genuine interest, not just reluctant acceptance, validated my plan further and continued to help my confidence grow. Now, I only had a few short weeks' notice to work out.

During that time, I worked to refine my first blog post and make final tweaks on my website. After a couple weeks more work and plenty of revisions, the very first post was ready to go – I was as happy with it as I knew I could be.

I hit publish.

Publicly committing to the challenge was the final step that wouldn't allow me to go back, and **that** was the point; if you are about to make a rather bold and intimidating life decision that you are not entirely sure you will follow through on, tell as many people as possible so they can hold you to account.

At first close friends read it, then my wider friendship circle, then acquaintances, and then people I had only heard of by name. Finally came the people whose names I didn't recognise. Over one thousand people read it in the first few hours. They started by posting supportive comments, saying that they wished they could do this too, others started messaging me directly, asking countless questions about the project and asking for advice. All said how much they could relate to the issues and emotions I'd identified. Being exposed so publicly made me feel deeply vulnerable, but acceptance from my peers – other millennials – further entrenched my commitment to completing the challenge.

Working out the last week of my notice period, colleagues began to ask what I would be doing instead. As I started to explain, word got around that I wasn't quite going straight into another job. I got tens of emails from people I knew and plenty that I didn't to say how much they wished they could do the same and how much they felt the same way about work. Many asked for advice on their own predicaments and others have enthusiastically asked to follow my entire journey.

And just like that, the project grew from a personal quest for career happiness and fulfilment to promoting those as a standard, rather than as an impossible ideal, and advocating for more diverse career education for young people.

That afternoon, I packed up and left the office for the last time. The last few pounds of weight that my subconscious had placed on my shoulders had finally melted away.

As I walked out that door that I had paused in front of so many times before, I didn't look back.

It was terrifying. And liberating.

Points for consideration

- Do things your way.

- Those who are unsure of their career aspirations are one of the least likely to receive careers guidance.

- What we think we want as teenagers is often vastly different to what we decide we want in later life stages.

- Your career options are not one dimensional, finite or linear.

- We need the ability to try out as many of our career interests as possible without the need to prove a longstanding commitment to it.

- Careers education should not be an added extra.

- Work experience isn't just for teenagers.

- There are so many different possible selves to choose from.

- It is all too easy to romanticise and idealise some careers.

- Feeling like you have nothing to lose makes you far more open-minded to the odd crazy idea.

- If you are about to make a rather bold decision that you are not entirely sure you will follow through on, as much as you want to, tell people so they can hold you to account.

- Careers should be like dating; almost none of us marry the person we first meet, so why do so many of us pursue the very first career we try?

- Job happiness is good for you.

- Being happy in your workplace is good for business, dramatically so.

- Career happiness is an exception that should be the rule; careers should enrich life rather than detract from it.

Questions to reflect on

- What is it, exactly, that you hate about your job?
- Do you need to change job or change career?
- If you could leave your job without the immediate need to start a new one, what would you do?
- If you could choose to try out any careers, which ones would you choose?
- What version of yourself do you see, when daydreaming? Who do you aspire to be?
- How important is it to you to know yourself, to really understand who **you** are and what **you** want? Which of your possible selves will make the greatest positive change in your life, or the lives of others?
- When you are in your eighties, what do you think you will remember with pride and pleasure?

ARCHAEOLOGY

I turned up sleepy-eyed at Cluj-Napoca airport, which I did not know how to pronounce before arriving (I later learned it was Cl-oo-ge Nap-oh-ca), expecting to see Dracula and Vlad the Impaler style tourism everywhere. Whilst there may well be parts of Transylvania where this is the case, I am afraid to say I saw not a suggestion of oversized human canines.

Instead, I spent two weeks trying out my childhood dream of being an Archaeologist in Sarmizegetusa (pronounced Sar-meez-eh-ga-two-za, affectionately nicknamed Sarmy) on an excavation of the Governor's Palace at Ulpia Traiana Sarmizegetusa, the capital city of this area of the Roman Empire.

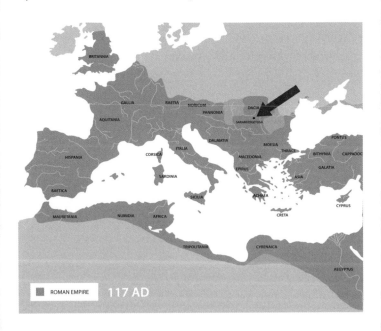

I was part of a European-wide team, and unsurprisingly the only member of the British contingent to have never participated in an excavation before and to have no idea what I was doing. There initially was very little explanation from the excavation supervisors, partly due to a language barrier. It was essentially 'here is a shovel and pick axe – dig down there'. It was manual labour under the mid-summer's sun. It was hot, sweaty and hard graft. I learnt that this excavation didn't have the funding for diggers or any other large equipment – that is what we were there for, for now.

During these first days I questioned what I had gotten myself into, standing in a muddy hole in rural Romania. Beyond the standard existential crisis that comes with quitting a promising career with no alternative plan – by now a normal thought – I questioned whether archaeology was right for me. Did I really want to spend my life digging holes in the dirt? Whilst I was enjoying being outdoors and the physical nature of the work, it was far from intellectually stimulating or inspiring.

However, some noticeably improved biceps, and a lot of sweat, toil and mud later, I learned that all this hard work had been needed as the top meter of soil was part of several 'disturbed' layers, meaning the artefacts in the grounds were not in context due to digging or farming from the interceding 18 centuries. Therefore, we needed to dig solidly to reach the lower layers, as they were far more meaningful.

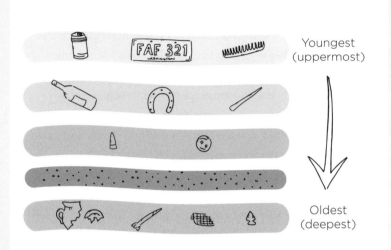

Youngest
(uppermost)

Oldest
(deepest)

Once I understood the reasons for the hard graft and when we finally reached the right layer, several meters down from the surface, my perspective changed completely. Within a few hours an oil lamp, a hairpin and a ceramic face appeared, along with pottery, painted plaster and bones aplenty. A few of the floor tiles were found with animal paw prints in them, from 1,800 years ago.

This was far more what I had in mind and I found it instantly rewarding – all that digging was worthwhile. The idea that no one has seen this object since the 2nd century AD, and that I had the honour of being the first person to have touched it since then, was more than enough of a romantic thought to capture my imagination.

But more than anything else, it was the human connection that I found most inspiring, as whilst the architecture tells us a huge amount about Roman society, bricks and stone do not hold quite the same amazement as placing your finger over the fingerprint of someone who lived 1800 years ago. Seeing how people lit their homes and tied up their hair, how they painted their rooms, left messages and graffiti scratched into the ancient plaster connects you to history in a way that no book can.

It is a special experience when your trowel first touches an artefact in the soil and is completely different to seeing it behind glass in a museum cabinet.

How well do I fit archaeology?

Archaeology was a fantastic first placement – it allowed for a substantial amount of time outdoors as well as being highly intellectually stimulating. I could travel the world when excavating, and there would be plenty of problem solving and variety. There are huge advances in the uses of technology in archaeology, with innovations starting to change the way excavations are being done, something I would really like to learn more about.

But I had to question, as an archaeologist would I be adding real value to society? Would I make a difference and leave the world a better place? Unless I discovered the next Tutankhamen or Pompeii (I think we can assume I won't), I was not certain that I could answer 'yes'.

During one of the many summer thunderstorms that rolled over the Carpathian Mountains, as we sheltered under the tin roof that was meant for shade, I asked the professional archaeologists I was working with what their answer to that challenge would be. Among many reasons, they pointed out that I would be working towards preserving the cultural heritage of a society and could contribute to constructing the narrative of the site, culture or even era I was studying and lecturing on, which would be there to inform future generations.

They explained how widely this profession could impact. Archaeologists often provide evidence in court for helping local communities prove they are native in North and South America, which can grant them a protected status and give them land rights. Archaeology can bring tourism into an area, along with the associated jobs and money as local people help out on digs and provide services to the often, sudden influx of tourists. This is beneficial to everyone involved as it strengthens community ties as well as increasing the chances of the site being properly protected and preserved for future generations. Then there are the fun things like advising in TV and film productions (or even participating, if you are on Time Team).

'Discovery! Variety! Being outdoors!' were just some of the reasons thrown at me when I asked some of the other reasons why they had chosen the profession. The mixture of practical and intellectual was also pretty high up. Money was mentioned, and the group laughed at the irony; archaeology is a not a profession you choose if you have expensive tastes.

One of the academics supervising the excavation gave me a more in-depth answer by telling me about her interest in stories. 'Not just in the names and dates, but in what actually happened and how people lived in a different era. I wanted to see what was next.' This I can certainly relate to. She then started explaining how she was also fascinated by 'mysteries, puzzles and detective stories'; she loved reconstructing a picture by finding the right evidence, and the final thrill of solving the problem. It turns out, to be Indiana Jones, you actually need to have a good dose of Sherlock Holmes in you. Makes sense.

For this lecturer, another major driver was the travel. Growing up in communist Romania with its closed borders, she had only been able to read about going to other countries. In the post-communist era as the borders opened, archaeology gave her access to the world and exposed her to people from different cultures and communities.

Finally, I asked the lead professor of the excavation, 'why archaeology?' He is a world-renowned archaeologist of the Eastern Roman Empire and is the type of person whose very presence commands instant respect. This is a particularly impressive trait, as he looks like the Father Christmas of archaeology – think St Nicholas in Indiana Jones' clothes. In a slow, rumbling voice he explained that every morning, even after a life dedicated to the study, he still thinks, 'maybe today I will discover something fantastic. Maybe today I will find something beautiful and unique, something that will completely revolutionise our understanding of this topic.' That hope has kept him going in the years in between those rare finds. This was a person who could not wait to get up every morning and do his job, despite having done it nearly every day for 50 years. That is an exception that should be the rule.

There were enthusiastic nods around our table, with everyone agreeing that this dream of finding something truly spectacular and game changing was what drove them. This is the feeling of longing for finding buried treasure and that is something that archaeologists (or, at least, these ones) get to have bubbling inside them every single day. How many of us are paid to feel that?

In the interest of not glamorising archaeology too much, there are downsides too, though many are true for academia more widely. Getting PhD funding can be a challenge and needing to do at least four or five years of further education on top of an undergraduate degree means that many of life's milestones are delayed. Getting a mortgage is difficult and many choose to put having children on hold until they are more financially secure. Academia can also be pretty cutthroat as work is often personally driven and you are in direct competition with your peers, though this varies depending on subject area. There is also the option of becoming a commercial archaeologist, conducting fast-paced excavations ahead of building projects by private companies.

There is something very human about wanting to know your roots, where we are from and how similar or dissimilar we are to our ancestors. This knowledge is intrinsically valuable, and archaeology is one way of showing that. In a way, that is far more of a strategic or 'bigger picture' contribution than helping those alive in my lifetime.

The final question I had to ask was whether I was passionate enough about this to dedicate my life to it? I now know that for Roman Archaeology, the honest answer is no. But there are other areas that fascinate me, so it's in the maybe pile for now. Who knows, we don't yet have an Egyptologist Mary Beard...

CHAPTER THREE

ON A METHOD TO SOLVE YOUR CAREER MADNESS

on crafting your own path:

there are not more than five musical notes, yet the combinations of these
five give rise to more melodies than can ever be heard.
there are not more than five primary colours, yet in combination they
produce more hues than can ever been seen.
there are not more than five cardinal tastes, yet combinations of them
yield more flavours than can ever be tasted.

– sun tzu

Those overwhelming feelings of escape and relief have never really left. They implied that I had felt imprisoned before, even if I hadn't been able to articulate it at the time. The next few months were the first taste I would ever have of being my own boss, of deciding what I wanted to do and when. On weeks without placements, I could decide where I worked and what hours I would do. That sense of independence was a little intoxicating, difficult to give up once you have tasted it. The idea of having no boss, no supervisor, no one at all to hold you to account other than yourself is daunting to begin with if you have only ever lived life with teachers then bosses. You get to call your own shots.

I woke up at half past eight on my very first Monday morning, beaming. I didn't have a placement organised. Theoretically, I didn't **have** to get up at seven in the morning anymore; I didn't have anywhere specific that I had to be by a certain time. I didn't **have** to get on a sweaty, fetid train and I didn't **have** to get through 200 emails. I could stay in my pyjamas all day if I wanted to. It felt like I was breaking all the rules of adulthood.

My conscience rattled loudly though, before I got too comfortable. My concerns on that first Monday, were that I wouldn't be self-motivated enough to work as hard as I would have if I had still been in a full-time job, especially once the novelty of quitting had worn off. Having a slow Monday morning was an acceptable thing to do as student, but not now. There was a lone devil on one shoulder who was chattering away, telling me that I could just as easily start tomorrow, that I could binge watch a series of Family Guy at ten in the morning today and there was no one to stop me. Strictly speaking, he wasn't wrong...

Panicked at how easily I could lead myself astray, I got dressed, grabbed my laptop and headed out to a nearby café to send out speculative emails for potential future placements and get started on writing another blog post. No working at home for me quite yet.

On day two, I decided to try working at a co-working space – a shared space of independent workers – in London that Facebook Adverts had (very creepily) suggested I take a look at. The space was filled with entrepreneurs that had created a community for themselves and other very early stage start-ups. It threw me into an office-based rhythm that was good for productivity and gave me some semblance of 'normality' to help to ease the transition. But on my commute home, with my face yet again in a taller person's armpit, I realised that my fears of being solely responsible for myself had driven me to start doing all those things that I had hated so much.

What was I doing!?

I could be productive on my own. I could create my own normality. It was dawning on me that learning to have faith in myself was going to be a rather larger part of this journey than I had bargained. This experiment wasn't just about career choices, it was also about self-reflection and figuring out who I am when there isn't anyone else around to give me the answers. There was no one to label me, no one to put me neatly in this box or that category. There was no one to tell me what I should be doing, what my targets are and what my next steps should be. There was I and I alone, and I didn't know what was coming next.

This would have terrified the Emma of old. Uncertainty – an open-ended black void of unfilled time. For the first time in my life, I didn't know exactly where I was going to be and what I was going to be doing on Thursday at three in the afternoon, or next Thursday for that matter. This time next month was unknowable. This time next year was wholly unimaginable.

Life up until this point had been about careful planning and precision. Every decision was designed to move you one step up in the game, one rung up the ladder, one this, one that. Relentlessly forwards, onwards, upwards. When you are swinging with such momentum, the idea of that stability no longer being there is sickeningly inconceivable. No more games, no more ladders, no more momentum.

Over the next few weeks, the way I had always thought started to change. I began to realise that it's OK not to know what comes next. Not only did I start to accept it, I started embracing it.

Slowly what had been a dark and terrifying void was morphing into a blank canvas. Voids suck you in and pull you down. Canvases, however, are for filling and creating. My mindset was metamorphosing. I began to welcome the idea that I didn't know what was coming next; I started to revel in it even. Not knowing suddenly became endless opportunity. Unknowable spontaneity became enticing, exhilarating. Instead of being pulled down into that void, the New Emma was being pushed up in front of a canvas that she could paint however she chose.

Only a few weeks before, I had found myself excavating Roman ruins in Transylvania. The sheer randomness of the experience was thrilling. This time next month, I could be trying out any one of those visions I had of Emma The Something Spectacular. I didn't know which one, what I would be doing or where in the world I would be, but that was what kept me up instead now. No longer did I lie awake dreading dawn; I started lying awake dreaming of the possibilities that the next day would bring.

And indeed, it did.

One night later that week I went to a friend's flat warming party. There was wine. I drank the wine. As previously mentioned, I'm not exactly commanding in stature, which means that I also can't hold my alcohol. It's a sore point. On this occasion, however, being a little tipsy on a weeknight worked in my favour. In my merry state I started enthusiastically chatting to another woman standing near said wine. I started telling her all about what I was doing. In honesty, the details are a little hazy, but it ended in her general approval and taking down my email address. She said something about how a friend of hers would find this all very interesting too.

The next morning, I awoke to an email in my inbox from The Daily Telegraph. It turns out that her friend was a journalist who would very much like to write a feature about what I was doing. That was a first. It was also my first introduction to the power of informal networking, a lesson that the whole of the next chapter is devoted to, incidentally. An interview was scheduled for a few weeks' time.

Over the following days, my time began to miraculously fill up. Some of the people I had emailed had started to get back to me. A few thought it would be a great idea to meet for a coffee and others offered me placements within their organisations. I had made the first few dabs of colour on my slightly less blank canvas. The next dab was bright blue; it involved a plane journey to an island in the middle of the Mediterranean Sea to start my photography work experience.

After two weeks clicking away in Ibiza, I had two placements under my belt, it was becoming apparent that I needed some way to figure out how to choose between what was hopefully soon to be several 'yes' careers. Whilst the placements that I had done so far consisted of a 'maybe and a 'no', I was hopeful that I would soon start filling that elusive third category. I wanted a more methodical way of figuring out which ones to pursue more seriously, as opposed to only going with my gut; instinct would certainly be part of the decision-making process, and yet it seemed wrong for it to be the sole factor. But how do you know what's important to you?

At all previous points in life, I have tried to make myself fit into a career that I have been aiming for. I have consciously worked towards gearing my skillset to things that I knew would be desirable, regardless of whether I might be naturally good or even like them. Yes, I was mostly drawn towards careers that played to my strengths, but in a much more ephemeral way. This was because, until now, I would not have had any serious experience in the workplace to draw upon. I was a school pupil then university student who was talking about what I might want to do in a totally abstract capacity. If I would have said at age 16 that I wanted to work as a journalist, for example, it would have been because I was good at writing essays for schoolwork, rather than because I had a serious idea of what was involved in that career path, and how it compared to other options that also involved writing, in all its different forms. Choosing a career up until I actually entered the workforce at age 22 had been based on guesswork and assumption.

The work experience and internships that I had up until this point weren't too much better, as my only thought was that I was simply lucky to be there. It never occurred to me to consider whether I was actually a good fit for them. I was there because I knew I had to do an internship and it 'looked good on my CV'. As internships were nearly as competitive as getting the actual job, so the pressure that came with managing to win a place meant that considering whether you enjoyed it or not wasn't really relevant, you were just 19 and astounded that you had even been chosen. If you dared voice any degree of dissatisfaction, another willing young person could quite easily replace you. In London, that meant working as an unpaid intern cost the intern on average £1019 per month, or £827 in Manchester.[42] You either had to rely on your parents for financial support into your 20s or work a second job in the evenings and on weekends to help pay for you to work in your internship – often a bit of both.

Of course, this meant that elitism is rife; walk into many city-based internship schemes and people from fee-paying schools are much more highly represented than the national average, which follows through to graduate jobs. On average, they get 70% of the most lucrative graduate jobs, despite making up 11% of the candidates.[43 44 45]

The millennial generation has grown up in the shadow of financial recession; we were mostly at school and in higher education when we first heard the words 'credit crunch' and started to see news headlines telling us that there was the highest level of youth unemployment since records began. Many of us, especially those who were entering the workforce during the recession, had to be thankful for any job they could get, often ones that they were over-qualified to do. Even now, 51% of jobs that graduates are in are not actually graduate level jobs.[46] Whilst the labour market has thankfully improved in the last decade, the mentality of young people remains nervous, remembering the experiences of parents, family and older siblings during the bad times just when we were on the cusp of maturity.

All of this meant that when I sat down to think what I wanted from work, I drew a blank. It wasn't a question I had ever been in a position to ask before. What I wanted from work, rather than what an employer wanted from me, was not something that I had ever been asked before. It seemed odd now that I looked at it from this perspective, maybe, perhaps, even a little sad? I had been prepared to dedicate my entire working life to a career path without ever having stopped to think about whether it might give me what I wanted, beyond making an abstract positive difference. I now knew what I didn't want which was a good place to start, but that's not always the same thing as knowing what you **do** want. I needed to build on that to figure it all out in a bit more detail.

To start addressing the problem, I wrote down all the things I could think of that I wanted from work and to force myself to write it without any specific jobs in mind, if there were no limits and money wasn't an issue. This was almost like automatic writing, when you let the pen carry you across the page.

Who am I? What do I like doing? What makes me happy? They are all big questions to answer.

What came out of that exercise wasn't a list of skills that you would see all in one job advert – although if you do, call me! There were a few more traditional skills, but there were also environmental and lifestyle aspects too.

PRIMARY AND SECONDARY CAREER ATTRIBUTES

PRIMARY

PROBLEM
SOLVING

MAKING A
DIFFERENCE

TRAVEL

THINKING
STRATEGICALLY

SOME NON-
DESK BASED
WORK

INTELLECTUALLY
STIMULATING

SECONDARY

PERSONALLY
ADDING VALUE

CREATIVE

INNOVATIVE

VARIETY

There were some things that had inspired me to initially join the public sector, wanting a career that makes a difference by helping others, for example, as well as solving problems. It had also become apparent that I needed to work somewhere that would allow me at least some time not spent at a desk or inside an office. Travel was also something that I wanted to feature as heavily as possible; being paid to spend time abroad is something so many of us dream of. Alongside this was variety, again something that I had learnt that I needed to keep me engaged for the longer-term. Turns out I'm not one for longstanding routines, who knew!

Then there was seeing the bigger picture. I'm aware that I'm much better working at this end of the spectrum than by doing something that requires me to pay very close attention to detail. Just as importantly, I really enjoy taking a more strategic, holistic and long-term view.

Somewhat interrelated was the desire to be personally adding value. Whilst I was not under any illusions that I would ever be irreplaceable in a job, I wanted to at least feel like whatever I would be working on made a real contribution to wherever I was working. Perhaps I could find this by working for a small organisation, for example?

Finally, I wanted to be doing something that had a creative edge to it and that was ideas driven. The right-hand side of my brain had been neglected for far too long and I missed using it, it felt like a muscle that was aching to be stretched again. This meant looking for somewhere that had a relatively flat and fluid structure, which would actively encourage the sharing of ideas from employees of all pay grades and had a focus on innovation. Creativity could be found through writing, design or a route that I had yet to discover.

Setting criteria to judge each job against helped me to be objective in my comparisons, and not be too heavily influenced by the individual companies and the people I worked with along the way, rather than answering the question of: 'what would it be like if I worked in this sector, more generally?' For example, in some jobs I found that I very quickly established a great rapport with those I was working with which made the hours fly by. However, when I came to the end of the placement, I had to consider if I had enjoyed it because of the work or because of the people and be honest about how much the latter could influence my opinion of the former. This worked both ways around, and there were certainly placements where I did not get on quite so well with individuals and had to make sure that this didn't negatively colour my view of the career itself.

Trying to understand exactly why or why not a certain career path was for me, was something that was especially brought home in my next placement, publishing, with a company called Bradt Travel Guides who publish – you guessed it – travel guides. Publishing turned out to be a no for me. But, at least this time, I understood a little more as to why I felt that way when I looked at my career criteria.

Now it's your turn.

When thinking through your own set of career criteria there are a few questions to answer to help guide your thinking. Consider these as impartially as possible, trying not to have a specific career in mind when answering. This is to ensure that you are not trying to (consciously or subconsciously) make yourself fit into pre-determined criteria; the spare peg in a round hole situation. Instead, start with an open mind and a blank sheet of paper. Whilst I came up with a list of ten, there is no reason that you need to, you could have six things, or you could have 16. I would recommend not having too many though, as it may leave you feeling more confused than when you started. Equally, less than three or four and you might find your options too narrowed or prescriptive. By approaching this with an open mind, it will help you discover career options that might not have occurred to you before, and to help you reconsider other paths that, on reflection, might not be such a good idea.

As you read through each of the questions, write down your initial responses after each one in your note book. They don't have to be your final answers, just some things you would like to think about in a little more detail. Following this activity, I split my answers into primary and secondary career attributes – my deal-breakers and my nice-to-haves. This will help to further organise your thoughts and allow you to focus on some things over others.

Why are you unhappy in the first place?

You have already answered this in Chapter Two. Go back and have a quick read of what you wrote down. This is your 'What I Don't Want' guide.

1. What do you enjoy?

What do you enjoy doing at work? Or, at least, what sorts of things do you imagine you could enjoy doing at work? Would it involve leading a team, or having the freedom to work independently? Is it words or numbers-based? Or do you like to schmooze clients?

What sorts of things do you spend your free time doing, through hobbies, socialising or volunteering, for example? Inspiration shouldn't just come from your working life.

Ensure you make the distinction between identifying things because you are good at them, as opposed to because you genuinely enjoy doing them; you need to be able to separate the two. Of course, hopefully they are one and the same, but this is not necessarily the case. Often part of our self-worth in education and then the workplace is tied in with what we get positive feedback for, as it makes us feel valued. At work, this can provide purpose and status, ultimately becoming part of your identity. Are the things that you want to list also things that you definitely want to continue developing?

What is slightly less simple is then deducing what is behind each of these interests. What is the attribute (for example, variety) or the skill (such as problem solving) that comes out of what you enjoy doing? For instance, my choice of creativity came from the fact that I have always enjoyed writing short stories, watching films and sitting down with a good book, and I am finding that I would like to increase the focus on this. That I want some time spent overseas and not at a desk originated from a love of travel in my personal life, along with a passion for the outdoors, especially for climbing mountains. Thinking strategically came from my Master's degree, which encouraged me to always see the bigger picture, something that I loved doing and which is also surprisingly hard to reverse.

2. What do you want out of work?

What do you want to get out of this? No, you aren't being selfish by asking this question, if you are going to be doing it all day long then it needs to make you go home happy. It could be responsibility, recognition or to constantly be learning something new. For many of us, it is about making a positive difference to the world in some way; doing something good. Scribble down all your thoughts.

A salary of a certain level is an obvious one for this and is often the first thing that comes to mind. Knowing this though, try to leave the finances to one side for this exercise as its inclusion can colour your views on the careers that are open to you; don't make assumptions about how much certain careers pay or don't pay, worry about that bit later.

3. What sort of working environment do you want?

This is easily overlooked, especially by those of us early on in our careers, but working environment matters and can make or break a job, potentially putting us off our career path entirely. This could be wanting to work for a small company, a large one or wanting to start up your own. It could be the inclusion of travel, of a commute that is a maximum length, the option to work from home, and what about corporate culture or the lack thereof? Think about how you work best, are you someone that would like more direction and feedback, or do you prefer to just get on with tasks? Do you want to work somewhere that has an informal dress code and a flat corporate structure, for example?

Now you have a few of your very first impressions written down, use a blank template – you can find an example in Appendix 1 – to collate your answers into a second iteration, giving a little more order to your thoughts by prioritising your previous answers into deal-breakers and nice-to-haves. This is a chance to clarify your thinking just that little bit more. Go back and change it whenever you need to reassess things. If you want to leave it for a few days to have some time to reflect further before coming back to it, great!

Compare your list of careers with your career attributes and skills list. Are there any glaring mismatches? Does your list of careers make you want to change any of your attributes, or vice-versa?

Once I had my two lists side by side, I looked back through my list of 25 careers and considered them through the slightly more analytical lens that my career attributes provided. At a second reading, some of the careers didn't make much sense anymore. There were a couple that I had always liked the sound of doing, but when I thought about it in more detail, they didn't really match up with many of the things that I wanted. Others didn't tick some of my deal-breaking boxes.

Bear in mind that there is a difference between disliking a job because of the environment and because of the actual work. If you are a junior doctor or a teacher, for example, it may not be medicine or teaching children that you dislike. Rather, it might be the problems that come with that profession such as underfunding within the industry, work/life balance or feeling undervalued, for example. Of course, it might be that you hate your profession too, and that's absolutely fine.

If you don't like the environment and know that is not going to change any time soon, it is OK for this to be enough of a push factor for you to want to leave. Just make sure you don't end up in another work environment that feels as toxic as this one does. Bear in mind, this does not necessarily mean you have to abandon health or education entirely, if you don't want to. It can be about finding other ways that you can use your skills within the industry in a way that you haven't so far.

To continue the analogy, as a doctor, you could decide that you would instead like to specialise in global health and international development or being a management consultant within the health sector. As a teacher, your skills can be applied to pretty much any industry you like and could involve teaching adults instead of children. In both scenarios, you could locum or be a supply teacher a few days a week to supplement your income for a while if needed.

Update any careers or career attributes as necessary in the blank templates in Appendix 2 and 3. Add in any other ideas you have had for careers you might like to try out too. These lists can change and grow as you do – just because you have written them down once, it doesn't mean that you have to stick by everything in them. Cross stuff out and scribble other bits in the margins. Highlight, add post-it notes and colour code. Make it your own.

I ended up buying a sheet of A1 paper and, assisted by a minor stationary fetish, created my own mind map of ideas for careers and different career attributes and skills that I wanted to focus on. Getting a clear picture in my mind, even if a fluid one, of what I wanted helped to organise my thoughts and further spur me into action. It gave me a stronger sense of purpose, strengthening my resolve in completing the challenge I had set myself as well as giving me a framework and structure to work within. I knew that intuition (and luck) would still colour my views of each career, but by being as objective as possible I wanted to try and better understand what it was that made me feel those reactions for or against a career. My gut hadn't exactly worked out all that well last time, so here was a chance to do things differently, to try and find some method in the madness.

Speaking to as many people as I could who loved their jobs and learning from their experiences further helped clarify things in my mind. In so doing, it also exposed me to jobs and careers that I had never previously known existed, reassuring me that there were almost infinite different combinations of things that I could do for a living, I just needed to narrow it down.

Interview with the expert: Magic Maker

Ducking out of a packed Baker Street station in the middle of the school holidays, I headed towards Madame Tussauds and even more rowdy queues of children. Mercifully, I was able to sneak around the back and escape the hordes – I had been invited for a behind-the-scenes tour of the famous waxworks. That was a ruse though; I was really there to interview George Paige, a 'Magic Maker' for Merlin Entertainment, the company that owns Madame Tussauds among plenty of other attractions around the world. One hell of a job title.

George's job is possibly one of the coolest sounding that there is, and as we try to weave past the crowds to get closer to some of the wax models, he begins to tell me his story. George studied law at university and whilst he enjoyed parts of it, other elements he deeply disliked. This is, of course, fairly common amongst students, but George felt he just couldn't continue doing the aspects he didn't enjoy. As we take a pew on either side of Yoda, George tells me that he went as far as dropping out of his degree and re-starting so that he could change the focus of his studies. The experience made it clear to him just how much he needed to enjoy what he did, quickly realising that this was far more important to him than the flashy city salary he had previously envisaged.

Watching the rabble of teenagers vying to stand next to the model of the Kendall Jenner, I ask George how he ended up with Merlin Entertainment. 'A mate sent me a link to the grad scheme, complete coincidence.' He says that looking into Merlin would never have occurred to him if it weren't for that. His fit with the company seems faultless, and he evidently loves his career.

With his arm slung around a Boris Johnson, who was placed a little too close to 10 Downing Street's front door, I ask him what it is that he actually does. George is a Group Intellectual Property Manager within the 'Merlin Magic Making Division'. When he mentions IP, I had a flash of concern that he was about to ruin my dreams of what magic making might entail, and yours too. However, I needn't have worried. George's role is to manage relationships with brands or individuals who are having rides and attractions created in their name. He then manages the creation and launch of each project – think Star Wars attractions, Saw roller coasters and A-list partnerships.

Could it be as good as it sounds? It seems that the answer is a resoundingly yes, but it's difficult to know for certain as George was sizing up Henry VIII at the time. He has worked in Germany on a Ghostbusters 5D interactive ride, in Madame Tussauds Amsterdam on a Marvel immersive figure set and launching a hotel with the BBC in Alton Towers – to just name a few projects over the past couple of years.

This all sounds very glamorous and it is easy to get drawn into the excitement, so I ask some more probing questions about exactly what it is about his job that he enjoys so much. George talks about how no two days are the same and that he is constantly meeting new people; yesterday he was at Alton Towers to show celebrities their models. The autonomy and flexibility are important too, as is his responsibility in shaping his own role. As his work is project-based, he gets to travel the world, having recently got back from a trip to Germany to launch a major ride. George is really 'not a morning person' but says that he has never struggled to get up for work in this job.

Of course, there is no such thing as a Prince Charming job – he confides in me that someone has to put mist on Justin Bieber's naked torso every day. I consider that this may not be such a chore in the eyes of many 14-year-olds. For George though, the negatives come down to office politics and the occasional bit of red tape, something almost all of us have to put up with and, for him, the good far outweighs the bad. He is someone who is fully aware how lucky he is that he has landed by pure chance in an industry he absolutely loves and frankly, excels at, straight out of university.

All in all, I'm pretty bowled over by what he does for a living, though having my arm around George Clooney is definitely helping.

Points for consideration

- You get to call your own shots; independence is difficult to give up once you have tasted it.

- This isn't just about career choices, it is also about figuring out who you are when there isn't anyone else around to give you the answers.

- Accept that it's OK not to know what's going to come next.

- Not knowing what comes next can create endless opportunities.

- You can create your own normal.

- Search for a job that you want to get up for, even if you are really not a morning person.

- Consider jobs where you are a good fit for them, not just the other way around.

- Setting criteria to judge each job will help you be objective in your comparisons.

- Self-awareness is key, as well as acknowledging your strengths and weaknesses.

- Speaking to as many people as you can will expose you to jobs and careers that you never knew existed.

Questions to reflect on

- How do you know what is important to you?

- What do you enjoy?

- What do you want out of work?

- What sort of working environment do you want?

FARMING

'If you like farming in January, you are meant to be a farmer.'

This was the advice I was given when arranging to work with Emma Collison at her farm, Moor View Alpacas. I tried to fight her logic and go in the summer months, when there would be a chance of sun and temperatures over 15 degrees, but in the end I couldn't disagree with her rationale.

So, a few months after first speaking to her, in mid-January, I drove through several hundred miles of rain to distant Cornwall. My data and phone signal slowly dwindled and died, until I was entirely cut off from the outside world. It was cold, dark and there was a considerable amount of mud.

The idea of working on a farm is not as random as it might seem for me. I have always been a lover of the countryside, animals and the great outdoors – my favourite childhood holiday was spent on a farm in the Peak District bottle-feeding lambs and being followed around by Border Collie puppies. It was all very idyllic.

Now as an adult thinking about careers a little more strategically, I know that I want something that includes at least some non-desk-based work, by which I really mean something outdoors. From interviewing Debbie Kingsley earlier this year, I learnt how entrepreneurial, creative and innovative farmers have to be in the modern day to make a sustainable living. My time with Emma Collison and her animals served to demonstrate this only further.

Moor View Alpacas

Emma imported 30 Valais Blacknose sheep from Switzerland several years ago, a rare mountain breed which had not been bred before in the UK. By breeding the herd to larger numbers, she has been able to sell many of them to other sheep farmers in the UK for profit – a Valais ewe can sell for as much as £4000. Emma sells the meat privately and is able to get a high price due to the rarity of the breed.

Then there are the alpacas. Emma owns around 30 that she breeds for wool, skin and meat – yes there are such things as alpaca burgers and sausages. She sells the meat to friends, family and local pubs; she gets the skins tanned and made into rugs, and the wool is spun into yarn and knitted into high-end luxury children's clothing for her clothing line, Moor Baby, as well as into duvet filling.

It is as much this entrepreneurial aspect of farming that I think I would enjoy, as the more obvious physical side.

The ups and downs

One aspect that was important to me was to understand more about where food comes from and that meant coming face-to-face with the harsh reality and the rollercoaster that is farming.

Whilst I was with Emma, the Department for the Environment ruled that all poultry nationwide had to be kept indoors due to a potential avian flu outbreak; a story all over the news in Cornwall, but one which slipped under the radar in Trump-spotting London. This meant that your free-range chicken and eggs wouldn't be classed as such anymore, with serious financial penalties to poultry farmers.

This massive potential for instability, and the impact it can have on businesses, seems to be common. On the second day I was working with Emma, she received a call from a farmer interested in buying £25,000 worth of sheep, a sale that would enable her to fully launch her children's clothing line. Two days later, she discovered that the farm she had just bought five alpacas from had gone down with Tuberculosis. Her new alpacas now needed to be quarantined and potentially culled. It's possible she won't receive any compensation, which would be a serious financial loss. No £25k sale.

So farming is a risky business and your success or failure can completely depend on external factors.

I did have the opportunity to visit a dairy farm that was booming, however. The Cornish Gouda Company was started by the 19-year-old son of dairy farmers, whose farm was on the brink of failure. He decided to diversify and produce the handcrafted artisanal Gouda, which have since won awards up and down the UK. Whilst the smell coming from the cow shed quickly indicated that I will never be a dairy farmer personally, I have the upmost admiration how successfully they have turned their business around to create a desirable product.

What did I actually do?

Much of my time with Emma was taken up with the day-to-day running of the farm and care of the animals. This meant feeding them, adding fresh layers of straw as bedding for the ewes and lambs in the barn, and best of all, bottle feeding a couple of the lambs. It also meant getting involved in some of the husbandry tasks, such as cleaning sheep and alpaca feet and cutting toenails, de-worming and giving vitamin supplements, as well as helping with the pregnant ewes.

It was mid-morning on my third day when Emma spilled another nugget of wisdom. With a lamb urinating down her arm, she said; 'farming is all about fluids.'

This should have turned my city-girl stomach and sent me running. But I loved getting stuck in. Even when it was raining, cold and I had an unknown animal product on the inside of my glove, I loved it.

I found the physical work incredibly satisfying, as well as thoroughly enjoying working so closely with the animals. I also loved learning about the farming industry and getting a better idea of where food really from, along with the challenges that poses.

This is the first career I have tried so far where I have sat back and thought 'this could be the one'. It combines the great outdoors and being close to nature with the intellectual stimulation of innovative entrepreneurialism. It is unlikely that I would be able to make a real difference and have a strategic influence, however it is not necessarily impossible – what I would learn about agriculture and animal husbandry could be transferred to the policy advice and international development worlds, if that was what I decided I wanted.

Whilst farming is not something I could realistically do right now for financial reasons, I would like to start by doing something, even if it's just keeping a couple of chickens.

CHARITY

This placement was with Advocates for International Development (A4ID), a global charity that partner commercial lawyers with international development organisations in need of pro-bono legal advice. This is an organisation that can make a difference to local communities as well as to governmental and international policy. This broad impact is part of its appeal.

As the ability to make a difference is quite high up on my priority list, getting some experience with a not-for-profit was important and I hoped that working with A4ID would provide insight into international development and the legal profession too (the straight and narrow could still be for me, you never know).

Whilst working there, I had the opportunity to speak to several of A4ID's employees, and so asked them about their backgrounds. Almost all of them had been solicitors and several discussed their disillusionment with working in traditional commercial law – many have moved to the charity sector so they could use their skills in a more meaningful way. Others had backgrounds based more in human rights law and a couple had previous experience directly in international development.

Changing careers

Elisabeth Baraka, Head of Partnerships and Legal Services, shared her experiences and career path. She is also driven by a need to make a difference, but growing up, had 'no sense of the wealth of opportunities' there are to do so. Not sure how to start, she became the fourth generation of her family to go into law.

After several years working in litigation, she made the decision to move out of private legal practice, studying for a Master's in

International and Community Development and beginning to work part-time for an organisation that provided services for the homeless.

Elisabeth spoke about the many professionals in highly-pressured and highly-paid jobs who say they do it 'for five years and then they will quit'. Except, in her experience, 'so few people actually do.'

Beyond this, she found that little from her school or university education prepared her for the need to creatively and innovatively solve problems – so much of education requires learning by rote with a minimal level of independent thinking and complex application of that knowledge. Over the course of her career, Elisabeth found herself having to retrain the way she worked to think more creatively.

This issue is part of the wider problem of the skills gap that government has identified with recent school leavers and graduates, compared to the needs of employers. Those of us who have just left education may know our facts, but often we lack the work experience to know how to apply these to work-based situations.

However, her advice to those looking to move into a charity or humanitarian organisation from a profession was to 'consistently follow what you're passionate about and you will get there'.

You should 'take that pay cut as soon as possible', as the younger you are, the less it will impact you. Taking a substantial pay cut when you have a mortgage, children and are accustomed to a certain lifestyle, is much harder than doing so before you have those financial commitments; it's 'easier to walk away from'.

Whilst it was great to understand how the organisation worked, I realised that I had actually been hoping to learn more about law and international development, rather than how to broker the relationship between the two. A4ID do not do the pro-bono work itself so my time with them was more about learning how a charity works from a more operational perspective. It was interesting to find out more about this area, as operations are the backbone that keeps any organisation running.

Whilst the work that A4ID does focuses on doing good, it does so at one step removed, in a more enabling capacity – it enables others to make the difference. I think I am looking for something where I can make more of a direct impact.

However, for someone already working in the legal sector looking to make more of a difference, this is a small but critical area that provides an alternative to traditional careers through a more nuanced aid perspective, along with benefit of the flexibility for a good work/life balance.

PHOTOGRAPHY

The smell of pine trees was the first thing I noticed about Ibiza, rather than the tequila that was conspicuously being spotted by the lads behind me. The days when partying in Ibiza sounded appealing are behind me.

My photographer friend, Marie, met me at the airport and piled me into her little yellow car before whizzing us off to her little flat next to a fig tree in fruit, far away from the clubbing strip in San Antonio. I would be spending a week working with her, and she had agreed to allow me to be the second photographer at a wedding the next day.

I had never photographed weddings before, or even an event. What photography experience that I had, came from travel and wildlife, with only the occasional portraits of the people I met along the way, and I certainly was very amateur.

Events are certainly very different to shoot; I had a lot to learn. You need to be sure not to miss anything, fully concentrating for at least eight hours, something that can be mentally exhausting. In a usual office-based day, it's rare that you are hyper-focused for the entire length with absolutely no break for food or to use the bathroom; it is broken into shorter bursts of concentration. As a photographer, though, if your mind wanders for five minutes, then **oops** that was the funniest joke of the best man's speech and everyone was laughing, or **whoops** that was your only chance to get a shot of bride's face during the first dance when the lighting was just right. This continuous level of intense focus was something I had not considered before. Whilst I was constantly engaged and always thinking about how to achieve the best possible image of that moment, and that certainly is a kind of problem solving, but it wasn't the sort that required me to really think through how to solve a challenging issue.

The right side of my brain got a workout as a wedding photographer, and that rush of creativity was exactly what I was hoping for. It felt fantastic to do something artistic and imaginative, things that I so rarely got to do in my previous roles. I certainly found it satisfying to know that I was recording the happiest day of someone's life and the photos I took would be treasured by the couple, their children and possibly even grandchildren for decades to come. I didn't know the family or guests but being surrounded by happy people is infectious and I came away grinning for them and may have slightly teared up during the ceremony when the groom cried as the bride walked down the aisle.

The wedding day itself is only a small part of the photographer's job. The rest of the week was spent narrowing down over 2000 photos to a much more manageable 200, and then editing the chosen selection to perfection. I needed an advanced Photoshop lesson from Marie. I learnt a huge amount about how to edit to a much higher standard than I did previously. Though, admittedly, after editing the hundredth photo, I did begin to find it a little repetitive, especially knowing that this was actually how photographers spend most of their time.

Whilst I love photography and know that it will be a passion for years to come, I just don't think it is enough to be my permanent career. Part of the point of trying so many different careers, experimenting and exploring my interests is to slowly narrow down my options, so discovering that a hobby is best kept as a hobby is no bad thing.

PUBLISHING

Deep down I was hoping that working for a travel guidebook publisher was the one. The elusive career I had been searching for. From the outside it seemed genuinely perfect, allowing me to write and travel, to be creative, innovative and solve problems.

I arrived in Chalfont St Peter, a cosy village in Buckinghamshire, on a crisp Monday morning to start work at Bradt Travel Guides, and for the first time I could feel the chill of winter coming on. My stomach was bubbling with excitement and apprehension – I was 30 minutes early as I so wanted to make a good impression for what was, quite possibly, my dream job. When I got into the much toastier office, I was shown a desk and promptly given a long list of simple tasks to get on with. Great!

I merrily got on with resizing photos and uploading them to the company website, I copied and pasted text to create articles, scheduled tweets for their account and did some proof-reading of manuscripts in the production process.

After a couple of weeks, I started to get used to the routine of working there and the rudimentary beginnings of their editorial process. I began to feel that editing travel guidebooks, as opposed to writing them, was that it didn't leave an awful lot of room for creativity, as the books were in a strictly standardised format, which is, of course, incredibly useful to the reader. However, editorially, this also doesn't leave a huge amount of space to innovate or vary things, things that I am beginning to understand that I crave.

It also requires paying intimate attention to detail, and I'm now fully aware that my strength lies more in 'seeing the bigger picture'. Self-awareness is a big part of this project, so acknowledging where my strengths and weaknesses lie and acting accordingly is a big part of what I'm learning. Add to this the fact that I'm very dyslexic and it could be a veritable recipe for an editorial-related disaster – well, not disaster, but a few too many typos in books. Maybe I should stick to the writing.

I also discovered that being a guidebook editor is almost entirely desk-based with relatively limited travel. This varies by publisher but made me realise that it was still far too office-based for me. The concerns I had about the working environment of a sedentary 9-5 job would certainly still be true if I chose this career path.

Towards the end of my time with Bradt I spoke to the commissioning editor, as I wanted to find out about other areas of the business. This editor was responsible for assessing proposals for new book ideas and writing samples, before negotiating contracts and finally working with authors to shape the structure and direction of each project, prior to them being managed within the department that actually edited the books. Within this part of publishing at least, this process interested me more and would probably be a better fit for my skillset, as it is ideas driven and has far more opportunity to think strategically about the business, something I am actively searching for; definitely a career idea to store for later.

As the point of experiencing the 25 jobs is to go and actually try the careers I had a mental question mark over, it would be far more of a problem to come away loving all 25, than just one or two. Learning that some of the careers on my list aren't for me is genuinely a helpful outcome as it narrows down my options in an informed way and allows me to make a choice based on fact rather than assumption.

And hey, I still have 22 others to choose from!

FILM EXTRA

There aren't many of us that don't secretly wonder what it might be like to be on the silver screen. Perhaps as the leading lady or the handsome hero, or maybe just in the background, to satisfy a curiosity for the experience itself.

I have never really given any serious thought to being an actor; at school, I was very happy to not be the centre of attention and until very recently the mere idea of public speaking was enough to make me break out into a sweat. The shiny, new, confident Emma decided to give it a go, and was given the chance to be a 'supporting artiste', which made the whole thing sound very professional and glamorous.

The excitement of the idea of being in a film meant I was perfectly alright with the 4:30 morning alarm on a weekend, and for once got up without needing to snooze my alarm six times. Getting to the unnamed central London location for six in the morning meant at least there wasn't any traffic either.

I walked into a large hall, filled with long rows of at least 20 dressing tables, with mirrors lined with lights on three sides; makeup and hair products covered the tables, exactly as you would imagine they should look like.

After a quick breakfast, I was whisked straight into one of the chairs and had my hair put in tight rollers and my nails painted. The idea of being paid to have a full makeover was definitely a positive one, especially when I had a night out planned later. I was then hurried over to the costume department and fitted into a floor-length purple ball gown with padded shoulders and sequins down the left-hand side, entirely appropriate for the scene being filmed that day. There were some surprisingly comfortable heels to go with it and an antique black feathery headpiece.

Back in the beauty chair and curlers out, my hair had shot up into tight ringlets, ending just below my ears. Sue the stylist had managed to tame this mess into a 1940s-style elegant mass of curls, in a way I have never seen my hair before.  With some deep reddish-purple lipstick on, it was time to get on set.

I had heard that extras can spend a lot of time waiting around on set and behind the scenes, so I had come prepared with some work to do. However, I must have been with one of the most efficient teams in the industry, as there was virtually no waiting around whatsoever. In the five minutes that I did have, an older gentleman in a crisp tuxedo sat down next to me and started asking what I did for a living in a deep Texan drawl. After giving up on trying to explain my life, I asked him the same question. By sheer coincidence, I had sat down next to the leading actor's father; his parents are extras in every film he's ever been in and follow him around the world from set to set.

I was later paired up with my 'date' for the scene who happened to be an old hand at being a supporting artiste, with several films and TV shows under his belt. Over the course of our rather intense ten-hour relationship, he dissected the film crew for me, pointing out who was the Director, 1st Assistant Director (AD), the 2nd AD and the several people who were 3rd ADs. There was the Director of Photography, the boom-holder and about 30 crew members who did everything from powder our noses in between takes to relighting our herbal cigarettes with a mini-blowtorch. All this showed how strictly hierarchical a film crew was, something I had no idea about beforehand; everyone has their own very particular job carved out, where they do no more and no less than that. The whole thing operated like a well-organised military machine, which perhaps explains the need for the strict structure.

Having the opportunity to totally transform yourself into a different person from another era is exhilarating, especially to a history geek, and I can easily see how people can end up doing this as a full-time career. Whilst I can imagine that the novelty of being an extra would quickly wear off, (this career ticked very few of my career attribute boxes), doing it every now and again as part of a portfolio career is definitely something I would enjoy doing as, hey, it was really fun.

But if nothing else, watch out for a long purple dress in The Guernsey Literary and Potato Peel Pie Society.

CREATIVE MARKETING

As it grew closer to the end of this journey, I had started to think more seriously about what I might want to do next. Working in a start-up in a creative role or industry (keeping it nice and vague for you for now) is high up on the list of things that I had narrowed it down to.

With this in mind, I spent a week working with Josh and Martin, co-founders of an online entrepreneurial magazine and a creative marketing agency. They began with the idea for a magazine about inspirational grass-roots entrepreneurs, aimed at students and other young entrepreneurs. After a couple of years in more traditional jobs following university, they packed it in and decided to start their own company, The Untold Journal. It seems it went pretty well; they were backed by Loughborough University and were able to take part in their early-stage start-up programme and have access to business funding. The first volume of the journal was well-received. The problem, however, was monetising it.

In the process of creating an audience for The Untold Journal, they had built a substantial social media following in only a few months – I have learned the hard way that this is far from easy to do and is often a full-time job in itself. It seemed digital marketing could be a way forward for the boys, leading to the creation of the Joshua Design Group.

A running theme of what I'm discovering during this project, is how much I enjoy working in smaller businesses and how different they are from organisations that are 440,000 people strong (the number of civil servants working for government). This point was yet again proved when I spent time working with Josh and Martin, as whilst they clearly worked incredibly hard, it was on their terms and in their own way. This meant starting later and finishing later. It meant socialising with other co-founders in the programme and learning from each other in a collaborative way I had not seen in bigger companies. Time and time again the benefits of innovation and creativity on a small scale were proven.

What did I do?

I spent my time with them doing what I seem to do best – writing. I helped out on the Untold Journal side of the business, spending time interviewing two other start-ups and writing their stories of success, as well as writing an article on start-up grant funding. I was uploading content to their website and they talked me through the creative marketing side.

I wasn't expecting to find it all as interesting as I did, which I guess is yet another example of why work experience is so important. Initially, I wanted to work with Josh and Martin because of the Journal but found myself wanting to learn more about the creative marketing side. I really enjoyed the challenge of generating ideas and liked helping businesses update their branding, showing them the benefits of social media marketing campaigns. There was a clear need for this sort of service. Many small businesses and even larger organisations are still discovering the opportunities gained from tapping into the potential that social media marketing offers, as well as on-trend branding and website design. I found it all rather exciting.

More than most placements, though, I spent much of my time simply learning from them and the other founders in the co-working space. Listening in gave me an insight into the struggles and successes of starting your own business, and it made me seriously think about starting my own for the first time.

This 'career' didn't quite fit neatly into the box of a specific job, as many others have, but it allowed me to learn more about content writing, social media, marketing and entrepreneurialism more generally. Clearly there would be a huge amount of creativity, innovation and opportunity to personally add value. Problem solving, variety and intellectual stimulation would also feature heavily too, as work is all project based and would enable me to really think.

Then, there are the question marks. In terms of thinking strategically, it would be 'yes' within the business itself, but not so much in terms of the bigger picture of influencing across an industry, or at least not in the early stages. Travel and non-desk-based work – again, yes as you are visiting clients and potentially filming or photographing for them, but I didn't get the impression that this is a big part of the job and visiting clients in the UK isn't quite what I meant when I said travel. That being said, if I worked for a larger marketing agency or as a small business grows, perhaps there could be opportunities to work internationally.

Finally, I don't think I could claim a tick for making a difference in the social impact sense. Again though, if you could work for a larger agency and specialise on working with charities, then in a small way you could say you were making a difference, for example by increasing donations. All in all, I loved my time with Josh and Martin, both from the marketing, magazine and general start-up perspectives. It got me thinking – is starting a business something I could do myself, where I could embrace all of the different career attributes that I'm searching for? Maybe total self-employment is the answer…

TV PRODUCTION

After trying my hand at being an extra in a film, I went behind the camera to give TV production a go. Raw TV specialises in drama and documentaries, tackling issues from cyberbullying to women in prisons to the race for the white house.

Based in Shoreditch, obviously, Raw looked cool and full of hipsters right from the off. I will admit to borrowing my much more fashionable younger sister's clothes for the week. I am an avid consumer of documentaries and dramas and have long been curious about how they are made. My base line of knowledge on this? Absolute zero. Fortunately, there was a very kind member of staff on hand to run through the basics with me.

Programmes start somewhere in the development team, the people who are constantly coming up with ideas, researching them and writing treatments on each. A new word for me too. A treatment is essentially the blueprint for the TV show or series, a brief outline that's only a few pages long to give an idea of what the show would be about. These are then pitched to channel commissioners. I had sort of assumed that broadcasters like the BBC, ITV and Channel 4 created their own content, it turns out this is mostly not the case as this is the role of production companies.

From here a channel commissioner will say 'yes – full commission' (very unlikely), 'no' (much more likely) or 'here is some money to explore the idea further', which is known as 'funded development'.

From here the project is moved from the production company's development team to its production team. Freelancers are hired to work specifically on each project, meaning the TV industry is very fluid with jobs – most members of staff are not permanent but are on contracts that will only last for the duration of the project. In that sense, job security is low, but that allows for a huge amount of variety and diversity, both creatively and in terms of meeting new colleagues, which is great for someone who doesn't want any two days to be the same.

I spoke to Kirsty Garland, who has a long career in the industry, having had the opportunity to work on projects ranging from 'the British Gymnastics team in the Beijing Olympics to Pink Floyd to abortion'. She felt it was a 'unique privilege' to be able to speak to people about things that matter most to them, through the casting process and by working with those who have been cast for a show. People trust you to tell their stories, with that comes certain ethics and morals, and there is an honour in doing so.

What did I do?

I spent my time rotating between several different teams, helping out in research, casting and as a general runner. For development, this meant fleshing out ideas that the team were already working on by researching them in more depth.

Whilst in production, I helped put out casting calls through relevant social media groups and interviewing potential cast members. No spoilers though, I'm afraid! As I runner, I manned the phones, booked very last minute hotel rooms and sourced props ranging from wooden benches to lamps. The extent that you are personally adding value though is debatable as I found myself asking what is it that I can bring to this role that would change it for the better. Due to the sheer competitiveness and fluidity of the industry, it did at times feel like people were replaceable.

Perhaps this also contributed to the strictly hierarchical nature of roles within the industry. This is certainly necessary to an extent, as a production is ultimately an incredibly complex project that needs to be managed to tight budgets and deadlines – there isn't much room for error. This filters down the ranks as all too often people simply do not have the time to engage with the ideas of those below them. There was certainly a feeling that you need to prove yourself by 'doing your time' at the bottom before your ideas – or by extension, you yourself – would become valid.

As with many jobs, sometimes it is what you make of it. You can choose to work towards projects that involve plenty of travel to exotic places and/or on documentaries that make a tangible difference off-screen. One production assistant told me how a previous project had featured the story of a young Syrian refugee who needed urgent cancer treatment. It was implied that he was not granted asylum specifically because of this as treatment would have cost a substantial amount. After the documentary was aired, a crowdfunding campaign was set up by members of the public – the money was raised, the boy received treatment and asylum as a refugee in the US and is now in remission.

So, all in all a mixed bag – a huge potential for opportunity and reward, but only with many years of round the clock work and very low pay doing jobs that, whilst fun, are unlikely to provide a high level of challenge and intellectual stimulation. I think maybe this one is not for me.

THINK TANK

Working in a think tank was something I thought long and hard about before quitting my permanent job. I honestly loved the idea of being able to while away time researching, analysing and writing about topics that fascinated me all day long. I think we have established by now that I am a bit of a nerd.

As policy-based institutes, think tanks provide expert advice and ideas on specific political or economic problems; they often cross the boundary of academic and practitioner, to be 'pracademics', if you will.

I spent a week in June working with New Local Government Network (NLGN), a think tank which supports local government and their communities to have forward thinking conversations about the sector. They tackle issues thematically, researching and publishing papers on areas like the integration of health and social care, affordable housing and the future of civil society.

Having worked alongside Local Government at a more strategic level from one of my roles in government, I could see that innovative problem solving would be welcome, so it was fantastic to see the 50+ NLGN member organisations working together with the researchers on practical solutions to big problems.

Speaking to NLGN's Director, Adam Lent, it was clear that there was plenty of cross-over with my goals. He spoke of how working in the think tank world is 'ideas-driven, creative problem-solving and about getting things done, all around a set of core values'. He also emphasised the partnership element, as think tanks are 'constantly collaborating with partner organisations and individuals, meaning that building successful relationships mattered', an aspect of this career that I had not previously realised. Above all though, he genuinely felt that he was doing work that 'made a difference by addressing pressing social challenges'. It differed to academia, as researching for a think tank was intellectualism with purpose and impact rather than for its own sake – though I wonder what an academic would argue?

Like any job, there are downsides to it too and the 'constant need to fundraise' is a big one in the think tank world – both in terms of individual research projects and for the organisation as a whole.

What did I do?

I arrived a few days after the 2017 general election, so the focus of much of my time there was what a Tory government, supported by the DUP, would mean for Local Government and the services they provide. So, for example, I was asked to write a paper on what impact the DUP's manifesto pledges might have on local government across the country, from council funding to housing, social care and education.

I was impressed (and admittedly a little annoyed, given their other more controversial policies, to put it politely) to find that the DUP actually had some pretty good ideas. Things like examining how to apply the most successful programmes of Adult Social Care from around the world, reducing homelessness and greater flexibility in what age children start nursery and school, for example, are policies I wholeheartedly support. The DUP also aims to reduce austerity measures, which may create some political space to debate an easing in national level austerity policy, beyond those which have taken place in the interceding month.

It reminded of my interest in politics (whilst at university, I had interned for an MP and loved it). Though it was all incredibly frustrating, as creating actual long-lasting change through Westminster is near-impossible, working for a think tank would allow me to be that one step removed, but to still have impact and make a difference.

I really enjoyed my time with NLGN – it was a small organisation where people seemed to genuinely get on well, how many of us have election parties with our colleagues!

Working in the think tank world would mean I would get to write and research for a purpose and have a social impact. This very firmly ticks the making a difference box, but also perfectly fits for problem solving, thinking strategically and being intellectually stimulating.

NLGN, in particular, would be great for innovation, creativity and personally adding value, as everyone's ideas matter and are valued.

There are still a few question marks though, especially over variety and travel, as well as non-desk-based work. I was with NLGN during an especially quiet period, where there was no events organised because of the election. A more average week would have included attending events, giving presentations and generally building networks.

You can't have it all in a job though, as we are all well aware, and again this is where it comes back to the idea of having a portfolio career. Finding a balance between different types of careers that fulfil you in different ways – think tank researcher and Forest School teacher, for example.

For anyone that is interested in this sector, though, Adam advised that written communication skills are critical, and are as important as research, as is the ability to network well to continue building and developing partnerships. If you are starting out though, 'find a specialism to build a profile and name around, and focus in on that at the start, then you can branch out more widely.' It is important to have a strong social media presence as you need to promote yourself as a researcher, as much as your ideas.

CHAPTER FOUR
ON GETTING 25 JOBS

the way of the world is meeting people through other people.
– robert kerrigan

Saying you are going to try 25 jobs in a year is a very different thing to actually doing them. The background organisation and administration of arranging and coordinating so many different placements took up at least 20% of my time and was not something that I had quite accounted for when I first set out on the journey. It was a major time commitment that took valuable working hours away from doing the actual jobs and running a blog.

Starting at the beginning, with a long list of careers to try and no obvious or easy way of doing them was intimidating. Whilst it never got less time-consuming, the benefits of being in contact with so many professionals started to pay its dividends.

How to network: on paper

The first four placements I got without too much difficulty by contacting people I already knew and by having a bit of luck, others were much harder to find and involved a lot of emailing to people I didn't know. This meant I needed to devise a cover letter along with my CV that would not be automatically thrown in the bin by every single one of the several hundred recipients.

The letter below is a standardised version of the cover letter that I used, and beneath it is a template that breaks the letter down into paragraphs, explaining what needs to go where and why. Knowing how to sell yourself well in only 200-300 words is an employability art form that takes practice before it is perfected. No matter which stage of your career you are at, it is worth spending time honing this specific skill; nail it and doors will open for you.

Sample cover letter: landscape gardening

Subject: Work Experience Request — 25before25

Dear xxx,

Last September I launched an innovative project to try 25 careers over the course of a year through short-term work experience, with the aim of promoting career fulfilment and advocating for more diverse career education for young people, I would love the opportunity to work with you as part of the project.

In terms of my background, [insert key points from education and career].

I am a keen gardener and would love the chance to explore this interest in a more professional setting. Having looked through your website, I find your designs inspirational, I especially love xxx about xxx. I would be very grateful for the opportunity to work with you or to shadow someone within your organisation for a week in July to learn more about what's involved in garden and landscape design on a day-to-day basis.

What I can offer in return, is writing up my experiences on my website and social media channels, to help inspire young people to consider this as a career path, as well as to promote your business.

Please let me know if this is something you might be interested in.

I look forward to hearing from you soon.

Kind Regards,

Emma Rosen

[phone number]

www.25before25.co.uk

www.linkedin.com/in/emmarosen1

Cover letter template

Paragraph 1: Why are you writing

Keep this as short as possible, preferably one sentence, or two at a maximum. This is your opportunity for you to grab your reader's attention. This first paragraph needs to tell them who you are, why you are writing and more implicitly, why they should keep reading all in one – it needs to tell a very short story and this is the hook. Having an email subject that states your request for work experience puts the why you are writing front and centre. It is your written elevator pitch and it is worth running it past trusted mentors or work friends. If you are making a career change, say so.

Paragraph 2: Why they should listen to you – credibility

Briefly outline any formal experience and/or qualifications. You don't need to spend much time going into all of your educational and employment history, just include the highlights in one or two sentences. These don't need to necessarily be directly relevant if you are trying to make a career change – as you can see with my example. It's more to show that you are at least a reasonably intelligent person who should be taken seriously. If you don't want to shout about your previous experience or qualifications, then focus on transferable skills like teamwork, written communication or analytical skills.

Paragraph 3: Motivation

Explain why you are interested in that career and why you are contacting the individual or company in particular. Research, personalisation and motivation are all crucial when writing this short section, so you will need to edit this for every single email you send, even if just by half a sentence. Be as specific as you can with personalising each email, it needs to sound like they are the only company for you. If you are stuck on something to focus on, try looking at the company blog, values page or social media for some inspiration. Again, this section should be no more than two or three sentences.

I have also included when I would be looking for work experience and for how long here, but you can add this in wherever it most naturally fits.

Paragraph 4: What you have to offer

Whether it's transferable skills from that project you did at university, or your deep understanding of using social media to engage an audience, be sure to show what you can bring to the table in the time you are with the company. We all have our own unique selling point and you need to use yours to your advantage. Think what the person you are contacting might have need of that you could offer.

Other points

When it comes to writing this, remember your ABCs: accuracy, brevity and clarity. That means no typos or grammatical errors; keep it as short as possible, cutting any and all unnecessary words; remove any ambiguity, the reader should not be left wondering exactly what you mean.

The sample cover letter I provided is 254 words in total. Don't go over 300. This email needs to be short and sweet to keep your reader engaged – much longer and you risk losing their attention. It needs to get to the point as quickly as possible.

Notice that I didn't include a CV here and have instead given my LinkedIn profile. This is specifically for work experience requests, rather than job applications. A LinkedIn page is quicker to look at and coveys the same information as your CV, and you get a notification if they have looked at your profile, so you know your email has been properly read. It also gives the reader an opportunity to connect with you on the platform.

You will also notice that I haven't mentioned money at any point in the cover letter. This is because, quite frankly, you should not expect to be paid, though some will offer to cover your travel and lunch expenses (and many did) – they are doing you the favour, not the other way around. I left the pay and expenses issue to the discretion of the organisation I was contacting as my goal was to work in so many different industries.

Informal short-term work experience or shadowing is different to a defined internship or offer of employment. Interns are legally classed as workers or employees; they should sign a contract and are entitled to be paid at least the national minimum wage and absolutely should be recompensed for their work. Whether this happens in practice or not could be the subject of an entirely separate chapter. Those undertaking short-term work experience and work shadowing, however, are classed as volunteers and usually won't sign any type of contract so aren't automatically entitled to any remuneration.[47] The type of work experience we are talking about here could range from an afternoon to a week, maybe two, at most. Don't ask for work experience or shadowing for longer than you are prepared to be unpaid for.

Who should you send it to?

This cover letter assumes that you don't personally know the individual or organisation that you are contacting; you are cold-calling them to ask for some short-term work experience. Wherever possible, research who the most appropriate person to contact is and email that specific person – you need a name. This may take some sleuthing. You may need to use publicly available information to work this out.

Start with the organisation's website and search through their team page. If you have no luck there, try looking at employees that you can see listed on the company's LinkedIn business page. Almost all organisations have a standardised email format, such as firstname. surname@abc.co.uk – you only need to see what this format is for one person who works there to guess the email address of the person you want to contact.

If that all feels a little too awkward to you, there are other options. For very small organisations, you can email the general 'info@xyz. com' mailboxes with 'FAO: Jane Doe – Work Experience Request' in the subject headline. Avoid emailing these general inboxes with larger organisations though, as your message is much more likely to get lost somewhere along the way, and often such inboxes aren't frequently monitored.

In a medium to large sized organisation, you need to find someone who is mid-level and obviously works in the area that you are most interested in; they should have the job title that you think you might want one day. Aim for someone too senior and, realistically, they are unlikely to have time for you. Too junior, and they may not be able to give you a well-rounded insight or might not have the authority to let you shadow them.

For smaller organisations and start-ups, though, throw that out the window. If there are fewer than around ten employees, you can aim for the top – the more senior end of the scale. Smaller organisations should work closer together and bosses should have personal relationships with nearly all of their staff. They should also be in a position to make quick decisions on whether to let you follow them around for a few days or not. I have had far more success with smaller businesses than larger ones for work experience placements, they are more likely to be able to be flexible and can benefit from the extra pair of hands that you would be providing.

How many people/companies should you contact?

In terms of how many people or organisations you will need to contact to request work experience to actually get a placement, it's a bit of a numbers game. For some industries, you may only need to email five, and in others you will need at least 50 before someone says yes. Aim for contacting 20 for each work experience placement as a start. The key is resilience and perseverance – essential employability skills in themselves, so don't let the rejection or lack of replies get to you.

If anything, aim for five to ten rejections. If you haven't had that many, then you either have been successful first time round or you haven't sent out enough cover letters yet. See rejections as part of the process, not as a marker of failure. Consider how many actual dates you go on out of five Tinder swipes; rejection is part of modern life so you just have to keep swiping.

If you don't have any luck after the first 50 though, look at your cover letter with a more critical eye and preferably ask the opinions of a few more critical pairs of eyes to see what you can do to improve it, the same way you might need to re-word your Tinder bio. It's also worth considering again exactly who are you sending your emails to – remember it needs to be people, not general inboxes, wherever possible.

Why a business should take on work experience candidates

This is otherwise known as 'other ways to convince a business to take you on for work experience'.

It's not all about corporate responsibility and altruism, although hopefully these things do play a part, but the reasons why organisations should encourage work experience are numerous. It is about investing it in the future economy, in new ways of thinking and new perspectives, as well as helping to narrow the skills gap now seen in many industries.

There are plenty of areas a business could benefit from work experience candidates, but this will make its biggest mark in IT and social media, skills which are often not a strength in employees of other generations.

From a somewhat more self-interested point of view, taking on people for work experience provides opportunities for your own employees to develop skills in management, leadership, communication and negotiation. It will help staff to upskill while feeling more valued and be more engaged.

In some circumstances, taking on young people can allow you to road-test products and services on your target audience, rather than paying for expensive market research.

From a recruitment perspective, taking on work experience candidates is a way to find a bigger pool of new talent without paying for services from recruitment companies. Word gets around too, and a company can foster a reputation as somewhere willing to invest in young people, helping it to be seen as future-facing.

Finally, taking someone on for work experience can also help them figure out if yours is an area that they **do not** want to explore further. This may sound counter-intuitive, but if we are talking about candidates who already have a level of professional experience, it means you will potentially avoid recruiting a permanent team member who quickly realises that this sector is just not for them.[48] It happens – falling into this trap is why this book has been written.

Allowing people to test the water of a career path first allows them to make far more informed career decision, based on knowledge gained by doing, rather than from assumptions and marketing campaigns. It's better for everyone involved in the long-term.

LinkedIn

This professional networking platform deserves its own standalone section as a way to reach out. Start by ensuring your profile is fully complete, up to date and specifies exactly what you are looking for in your summary (or in as much as is possible if you are doing this under the radar of your current employer). Do your research to create a list of specific individuals' jobs that you would like to get some insight into, make a spreadsheet with a link to their profiles. Get as many names as you can, which may take some time to build up.

Once you have this, upgrade your account to a premium subscription – this is free for the first month, and you set a reminder to cancel it before the first charged month kicks in if you don't want to continue it. A premium account allows you to directly message as many professionals as you like whose careers you are interested in.

As LinkedIn is more personal than contacting someone through his or her work email, adapting your cover letter to initially just ask to meet for a coffee (the best option) or arrange a video call (not as good, but still worth it). Don't start with an immediate request for work experience, it's much easier for someone to say yes to a coffee than to a week of working with you; coffees build rapport. Coffees confirm that you aren't a weirdo-stalker. Coffees will allow you to ask all the burning questions that you have about their working life, both the good bits and the bad bits, before then asking if you might be able to work with them for a day or five.

You can now send your adapted cover letters to your long list of interesting professionals with no restrictions; though send them a connection request to go alongside your note.

LinkedIn can also be used in your job hunt, when the time comes, and is now a core part of 21st century recruitment.

Two of the placements that paid off for me by using this tactic were landscape gardening and interior design. I spent a couple of days researching businesses that I could send emails out to and ended up contacting at least 20 for each one. The two who accepted me were one-woman businesses run from dining room tables; one was long established and the other was a recently launched start-up. Both were hugely creative and were completely unlike anything I had ever done before.

How to network: in person

You now hopefully have a few coffee meetings lined up from LinkedIn or through cold-calls.

Cappuccino in hand, you can now ask all the questions you want. The following are the ten general questions I asked at every networking meeting. They are relatively open-ended, leaving plenty of room for you to ask follow-up question on each topic. Use them to guide your conversation and adapt them for your own use and for each specific industry or career path.

1. What has your career path been?

    Start by asking about their journey in a more generic way. Chances are, you have already looked them up on Google and know the rough outline, but it's a good way to start the conversation and relaxes you both. They might come out with something totally unexpected that will catch you by surprise.

2. Why [this industry]?

    Learning about their motivation can help to give you an insight into your own drivers, which can open up a deeper conversation between the two of you on this.

3. What is your current role like? What about it makes you want to get up in the morning?

    An overview of their job is an obvious conversation starter. The second question, though, encourages them to consider all the highlights of their role. Some people will answer with very specific points about their current job whereas others may talk about more general attributes or themes.

4. What does an average week look like for you?

    Getting a sense of someone's day-to-day schedule will give you the best idea possible of what it would be like if you were working there. Often people answered with what projects there were working on. Whilst this is, of course, a useful part of the conversation, what you also want to get at is how much time is spent in meetings versus travelling versus feeding the animals, or whatever it might be. Asking this question often challenged some of my glamorising assumptions about certain jobs, making me realise just how much time was spent in meetings or at a desk, for example.

5. What are you career aspirations?

    This is to open up a conversation on where this career path might take you in the future.

6. Do you feel like you are making a difference in your job?

    You can replace this with the things that are the real deal-breakers for you. This was it for me.

7. Are there any expectations you had about this career path that you have found differed to reality, in both a good or bad way?

    Another point to challenge your assumptions about this career. This can be a difficult question to answer, so try giving an example of something that you had assumed to be true in this career. For example, corporate law has a reputation of very long hours and poor work/life balance.

8. What don't you like about your job/career in X? What are the biggest challenges? What are the compromises?

    This is one of the most important questions to ask. You need to know about this just as much as you need to know about the good bits; there is no such thing as a Prince Charming job. Every job has its downsides and you need to be aware of those things from the very beginning rather than five years down the line. This lets you make a more informed decision on if the compromises are worth it for you.

9. What skills are the most crucial to succeeding in this career? What type of person do you need to be?

Having an idea of the answer to this question will highlight any gaps you have in your skillset at the moment, showing what you might need to focus on building up. The second part of this question will give you some insight into the soft skills needed and whether the working environment is right for you.

10. What is the best bit of advice you have for someone looking to move into this area?

This question is, of course, very helpful. It will also allow you to segue into your elevator pitch and request for work experience, assuming that's what you want after everything you have heard, that is!

The elevator pitch

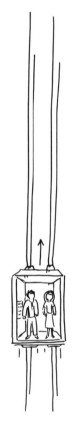

If you haven't fully already, now is your chance to powerfully and convincingly explain yourself to the person you are meeting with:

1. where you are right now.
2. where you want to be.
3. how you are hoping this person might help you get there.
4. why they should help you.

All of this shouldn't be more than five or six sentences, with the focus more heavily weighted towards the first two points. Phrase these last two more like questions than statements.

If you are considering a career change to something that is, on the face of it, totally unrelated to your current career path, then concentrate on your transferable skills. Don't bring up why you want to leave your current career but do have a positive sounding answer prepared in case you are asked.

This 30-second spiel is something you will hopefully have the opportunity to say again and again to all the different professionals you will be networking with in the coming months, so two points:

1. Practice this mini-speech so it naturally comes to you without memorising it word for word, just know the general points – the person you are saying it to will be able to sense that you are reading from an internal script by your tone and body language.

2. Be flexible with it. You should be able to adapt and tailor your elevator pitch to the specific individual you are meeting with. You can cherry pick the most relevant parts of your experience and skills, leading your pitch with those while down-playing or completely neglecting less useful experiences, unless you can find a way to link them via transferable skills gained. Give this a few minutes thought before every meeting until it becomes second nature.

Once you have this nailed, there are a few golden rules of networking to take note of: always come away with another person's name for you to contact, preferably two. John who does marketing for a gluten free subscription snack box start-up can't help you with your work experience quest, even though he has very kindly answered lots of your questions over a caramel latte. His old colleague at Graze boxes, however, might be just the person though and here are her contact details as John tells you to drop in his name when you get in touch with her.

Of course, coffee meetings through LinkedIn are only one way to network. Try going to school or university alumni events, industry specific events and fairs, join an inexpensive private members club and use Twitter in the same way you have used LinkedIn. Contact your school or university directly to ask if there are any specific alumni who work in your areas of interest and might be happy to be contacted. In short, shout about it to anyone who might be even remotely willing to listen.

The other golden rule is that you never know who knows someone. You might be having a haircut and your hairdresser or barber is particularly chatty. After a while, you find yourself explaining that you would actually love to change career and would desperately like to find out more about what it's like to be a coder for a tech company. Coincidentally, that's just what your hairdresser's best friend's husband does – here are his contact details, I'm sure he would be happy to talk to you.

Attending networking events on your own can be daunting. Not all of us are social butterflies who feel comfortable putting ourselves out there in a room full of strangers. However, whenever I am faced with that situation – which is very regularly – I always start by looking out for another nervous-looking person standing towards the edge of the room or inevitably near the wine, not talking to anyone. There is always someone else. If you are anxious, that's the person you go and talk to, as they are feeling the same way. You can make light of the situation, opening with, 'so you don't know anyone else here either?' This is your gateway into a conversation and to build up some confidence. Suddenly you are the one that's taken control of the situation and you will see a look of relief flash across the other person's face. If you run out of things to talk about or just want to move on to speaking to someone else (totally acceptable in a networking environment), you can always excuse yourself by saying you are going to find something to eat or in search of the bathroom.

As a general rule with networking events, no one knows anyone else and that is the whole point of them. This means there's no need to feel like you are interrupting if you try and join a group of people mid-conversation. Sometimes it takes a deep breath and search for inner self-confidence that isn't always easy to find. However, this is one of those 'live life with no regrets' situations; you will regret not going over and saying hello. Life is too short for regrets and opportunities left unexplored, even on a micro-scale such as this. Besides, you already have your elevator pitch prepared so you know what you are going to say. If you are really apprehensive, try prepping a few generic questions beforehand.

Even now, I still get a nervous kick of adrenaline on entering a room full of people I don't know in this sort of situation. I have done it so many times now though, that I'm able to harness that adrenaline and use it to force myself to go straight into the middle of the room. Where possible, I have done my research beforehand on the other guests attending, I have identified a handful of individuals that I specifically want to speak to and · I will go looking for them, ensuring that I will introduce myself before the end of the evening. As with all things, practice has certainly made it substantially easier – the more networking events you attend, the less intimidating they will become. Recognise that your first one might not be great and that is OK, because you know that your tenth will be.

When you are attending these sorts of events, get a few business cards printed and have them to hand for when you do come across people you would like to connect with after the event. It does feel old-fashioned but giving someone a physical reminder of who you are and your contact details is no bad thing. More importantly almost, is that they are likely to hand one back to you, enabling you to be proactive and follow up with them the next day to ask them if they will let you buy them a coffee and pick their brains.

With all networking that has gotten to the one-on-one-coffee stage, or at least the multiple email chain stage, it's important to focus on creating meaningful relationships rather than quick wins. They take time to develop and you should continue to foster them, taking an interest in people's lives. Like all relationships, both professional and personal, it's about give and take, and it needs to be two-way to last in the long-term. You might not be able to return any favours right now, but in six months, a year or even two years' time, you will be able to add value for them.

Keeping a little black book of all your contacts' business cards, alongside a couple of short bullet points on when and where you met them, and what they do is a good way to help you keep track and remember who you have met. You are really not a stalker – it's fine.

Job hunting and the hidden job market

The networking skills that we have discussed here can be applied to job-hunting more generally once you are further along in your journey and have a better idea of the career you want to move into. When you do get there, your strong networking skills will come in useful for both the advertised and the hidden job markets.

For advertised roles that you are serious about, always ask to set up a short call or meeting with the hiring manager before submitting your application. This will give you an opportunity to ask questions about the role to strengthen your application and to learn more about the team you would be working with and the working environment. Remember your list of career attributes; don't get drawn in by the rush of applying for something new. It also gives you a chance to get a better idea of how well you would get on with your potential future boss, and to ensure that they will remember who you are when your application does land in their inbox.

The 'hidden' job market refers to jobs that aren't advertised, and this accounts for 60-80% of all job vacancies.[49][50] These are the jobs that you find out about through your cousin's wife, that person you met at a networking event or an old colleague who you coincidentally happened to email last month and who you then went for a catch-up drink with. The hidden job market can feel nepotistic and there are, of course, issues with that. But, it is going on regardless and it's better to be in the loop than out of it, and the skills that have been laid out over the past few pages will help you break into those networks.

Networking like this is precisely how I arranged my next placement. After rather excitedly speaking to the journalist who interviewed me for The Telegraph, I followed up with her to ask all about her career and then eventually asked if there was any possible chance that I could do some work experience at the paper. It was time to give being a hack a go...

How to network: socially

So far, all the points that have been made about networking have been relatively traditional. One of the key things that I have learned, though, is to be as unorthodox as possible when networking, either for work experience or when looking for jobs. This led me to start using social media to my advantage while looking for placements, and later, for jobs.

The line between professional and personal on social media is becoming increasingly blurred, and it is up to you on the extent to which you want to embrace that. I started by tentatively exploring it, just to see what was there, but ultimately made the decision to cross that line and use it in the way many of my peers were. After all, they were the ones making connections and often getting jobs.

This is not to say that we should forget the value in face-to-face conversations, simply that this is another major tool in your arsenal that will hopefully lead to making those personal connections.

Cross platform

I started by, quite simply, writing a Facebook post, Instagram and a series of Tweets about what I was looking for, and using my social networks to reach my first and second-degree social circles. I also asked my school and university to post on my behalf to reach their audiences on social media too.

Timing was important for these; I made sure that I was posting at the time of day when most people are scrolling through their social feeds. Think about the times of day you most often look at social media and note how it varies by platform. Generally, for Twitter, it is best to post mid-afternoon as it is more likely to be used in a professional or at least semi-professional setting. Facebook and Instagram, however, are more personal, so go for lunchtime or evenings. Focus on Monday to Thursday rather than weekends when people check more sporadically.

I was surprised by the response, getting plenty of replies from people I knew and some I didn't, all offering help. Several people I hadn't seen since school or university days reached out, many of which I hadn't even been friends with. They offered to put me in touch with people they knew or even opportunities within their own workplaces. Time and time again, I was bowled over by their endless kindness and altruistic generosity that I was shown.

Twitter

As the year progressed, I started to use Twitter in a similar way to Facebook. I sought out organisations and individuals who used the platform as a professional rather than personal capacity and tweeted them, asking if I could learn more about their careers. As this was a public request, it put more of an onus on them for a response, rather than an email that could immediately be deleted or ignored. It can also be interpreted as flattering – you are publicly paying them a compliment by showing your respect for that person and their work. This is a strategy best used when targeting individuals or start-ups that seem to be particularly innovative and social media savvy, as opposed to larger organisations. Bear in mind that you are not tweeting them to ask for anything more than what would be an email exchange, phone or video call on the face of it. You are simply starting to open a professional dialogue to learn from their experiences, and you don't know where this might lead. Do not contact people who are using Twitter in purely a personal capacity.

If you are job hunting, as opposed to searching for working experience, there are certain hashtags to look out for. Most organisations will post a tweet about a vacancy they have just advertised.

Industries often have standard hashtags that they use to do this. Examples of common general hashtags include: #ukjobs, #jobposting, #hiring, #recruiting, #careers, #recruitment, #vacancies and #jobs.

Also monitor and save searches of industry specific hashtags. Some industries have well-recognised hashtags, such as #salesjobs, #financejobs, #hrjobs, #energyjobs, #devjobs for developers and so on. The search function on Twitter does not limit you to only searching for hashtags, try looking for '#legaljobs Manchester', for example. Research your areas of interest and discover what the most often used and relevant hashtags are.

Instagram

The rules are different for Instagram. Companies do sometimes use hashtags to advertise roles, but this is far less common than on Twitter and is limited to social media embracing sections of a smaller number of industries usually more creative and digitally focused ones. It is also harder to search for roles on Instagram than it is on Twitter due to the more simplistic search function.

Instagram's main use is networking. It is appropriate to Direct Message (DM) someone who runs a professional account or DM business pages, though try following them, liking and commenting on some of their content first to get noticed. If it is clearly a personal account, for example it doesn't list their job title or has photos mainly of their children, then respect their privacy and do not contact them.

Instagram is one of the more fickle platforms of social media; sometimes others view the number of followers as a measure of your 'value'. Hopefully, of course, this won't be the case with anyone that you are messaging, but unless you are an influencer yourself with several thousand followers, try targeting people or businesses that have under around 5000 followers. It is certainly worth trying your luck by messaging any relevant accounts with tens or hundreds of thousands of followers but manage your expectations on getting a reply.

Following on from this, if you are prepared to spend time building up your followers on Instagram, it can be a powerful tool. I receive far more messages through Instagram than I do through any other platform, which has led to several opportunities for collaboration with other businesses and influencers. To do this, though, you need to figure out what your niche is, which works best when pursuing a personal interest or hobby, or occasionally as a small business. That niche could very well be 'figuring out what I want to do' and taking your followers on a career search journey. It could be a 'life in a tech-start up' or 'my jewellery design business', but either way it needs to be personal, while still getting the messages across that you need to.

Used in the right way, it can make a substantial impact to your networks.

Facebook

For Facebook profiles, it's a resolute no on messaging people directly out of the blue. It is acceptable to contact someone, though, if they (individual or a very small organisation) maintain a Page or Group for their work or business that is regularly updated. Note: this is **not** their personal Facebook profile. Messaging them through this professional page is acceptable; I have both sent and been on the receiving end of this.

Many industries, especially those with a digital or creative focus, now have several Groups and Pages set up for people to network, share advice and opportunities in that niche. For example, for those who work in PR, film, digital marketing, content/copywriting, events, web design and photography, 'Creative Networking!' is a well-known, more general UK-based group that does exactly what its name suggests; it's a font of wisdom for contacts, ideas and jobs. Having gotten a freelance job through it myself, I really can vouch for it. There are plenty of industry-specific Groups and Pages that exist, and it is worth doing an in-depth search on Facebook and Google to find the one (or even better, the three or four) that is most relevant to you.

Look for Pages or Groups that have posts published several times a day and at least several hundred, if not thousands, of members as they will be the most active and, therefore, the most likely to be able to help you – and you are more likely to be able to contribute meaningfully to them. Messaging someone you have seen post in one of these groups for a related purpose is encouraged. Better still, though, try posting on Groups or Pages like these to ask for career advice or work experience.

This is how I ended up being an extra in a film. I started by joining Facebook groups for people working within the TV and film industries, put a post on one and was pointed in the direction of an extras' casting agency; I signed up on the spot. Several weeks later, I found myself on a film set.

After a run of placements back-to-back, I built in some time to do some much-needed networking for the next set of work experience, to work on my blog and generally take stock of everything that was happening. I also signed up for a one-day travel writing class. I was unsure where to start with that career and it was also one of the ones that I was most excited about so this was a small step forward.

The course taught me enough to write an article about a trip I had taken the year before to Turkmenistan. The end of the article mentioned the tour company I had travelled with and the logistics of how the hell you end up standing in front of a permanently fire-balling, gas-filled crater known as the 'Door to Hell' in middle of the Karakum desert.

After I had posted the article on my website and had some positive feedback from readers on it, I sent it to the tour company that I had gone with. Then something I had never dreamed of happened – the company liked the piece. They really liked it, it seemed, so much so that they asked if I would be willing to go on another trip with them and write about it, which could serve as my travel writing placement.

Well, yes. Yes, I would.

I did a real-life victory dance. Then I signed up to go to Venezuela later in the year.

Points for consideration

- There is no such thing as a Prince Charming job.
- Knowing how to sell yourself well takes practice, nail it and doors will open for you.
- Where possible, cover letters should be sent to someone specific.
- Ask as many questions as you can about what it's like to be doing each job.
- Get your elevator pitch right.
- Always come away with another person's name for you to contact, preferably two.
- You never know who knows someone.
- Life is too short for regrets and opportunities left unexplored.

Questions to reflect on

- Why are you asking for work experience?
- Why should they listen to you?
- What is your motivation?
- What do you have to offer?
- What is your elevator pitch?

TRAVEL WRITING
Mérida: Smoke Above The City

The city of Mérida is nestled high on a plateau in a valley that is edged by thick cloud. When I arrived, the city was engulfed in fog and the winds were high – a storm was brewing, both high above the city and on its streets, down below.

Mérida is Venezuela's Andean capital of adventure. Tourists have come for decades to go mountaineering, canyoning, paragliding and to escape the heat of the savannah and rainforests that cover the rest of the country.

First up at six the next morning was canyoning. Waiting in the hostel lobby, quarter-past six then half-past came and sleepily went. The phone rang at the reception desk, piercing the dawn silence. The guide had called to say that the protests and street blockades had cut off every road into and out of the city, he could not get in and I could not get out.

Not quite knowing what to do next, I headed out onto the streets in search of breakfast.

I only had to walk a couple of kilometres before I reached a roadblock; medical students from Mérida's university, many wearing pastel-coloured scrubs, were blocking a major city intersection.

At least 24 were killed in the previous two weeks, in violent protests across the country and in the capital, Caracas. Recently, they have been demonstrating against the government's failure to set election dates and President Maduro's anti-democratic moves to create an unelected body at the most senior level of Government that cannot be held to account. Venezuela is quickly sliding into dictatorship, and one that is armed with 5000 Russian surface-to-air missiles.

The economic issues, however, are even direr. Wages are impossibly low; a teacher earning $15 per month, an engineer on $60. Most essentials are rationed or extortionately priced, with inflation surpassing 700%. Products as basic as bread, milk and nappies are now rare luxuries. Toilet paper is completely unavailable. Poorer citizens can queue for hours to buy items at the state-set prices, but those who still work cannot afford the time to queue so are forced to buy products at up to ten times the price. 93% of the population have said their income is not enough to cover food and Venezuelans have lost an average of 19lb in the past couple of years from not being able to afford more than two meals per day.

Walking in amongst the two hundred students, there was a festival atmosphere. People were standing in groups; singing, playing music, painting faces, blowing whistles and waving flags. It was only when a motorbike tried to cross the picket line that the true nature of the demonstration became apparent.

Abruptly, the singing turned to screaming and the music stopped. As the disparate groups ran together to surround the driver, the whistles started to sound aggressive and threatening. Protestors urged the driver to turn back; he would not be allowed to leave the city today. As he refused, the screams grew louder and someone started throwing small stones. The driver was furiously yelling back, gesturing violently. A tall protestor at the back of the enraged crowd produced what looked like a gun with an ultra-wide barrel, waving it wildly in the general direction of the motorbike driver's head. I took this escalation as a sign that it was best to leave.

As I walked away, towards the bridge that led back into the city centre, something exploded. The sound and shock bounced through me, instinct forcing me to double over. Looking up, I could see smoke above the crowds and could hear more shouting. A motorbike with a terrified driver whizzed past me.

Turning a corner into the main plaza, the atmosphere changed again. Only a couple of hundred metres away, daily life continued as normal. Salsa music blared, street vendors were selling fresh orange juice, sliced pineapple and grilled maize arepas stuffed with melting cheese. Hawkers walked past with hot coffee and mangoes. In the cathedral, a graduation ceremony was underway for the other half of the medical students. The tempo of the lively horns, drums and piano just covered the screech of passing sirens and more distant blasts. But the red graffiti is what gave away many in the city's feelings; every wall was covered in anti-government slogans demanding for the President's resignation and labelling him a dictator, longing for the return of the long-dead Hugo Chavez and constantly calling for revolution.

Once one of Latin America's wealthiest counties following one of the largest discoveries of oil on the planet, the country has a huge amount of offer – it is one of the most bio-diverse in the world with hundreds of endemic species. It has the several thousand kilometres of Caribbean coastline, glaciers in the Andes, endless savannah plains and, of course, dense primary rainforest. Culturally, Venezuela is a melting-pot of Caribbean, Spanish, indigenous and African music, dance and art. Over 50% of the population defines itself as mestizo, of mixed descendancy, and as with much of South America, this is obvious just walking down the street.

But despite this, Venezuela is at a dangerous tipping point, and the tension is palpable. It feels as though only the smallest of sparks is needed to set it ablaze.

FOREST SCHOOL TEACHER

Back in January I was contacted by a Forest School teacher at Beechwood Park School, Hertfordshire. I had read the occasional article on Forest Schools and loved the concept, so was thrilled to be asked to come along and see what it was like in practice. A Forest School is an innovative educational approach to outdoor play and learning, which is used alongside the regular school curriculum and traditional teachings in a participating school. Sessions are set up for children of all ages to visit local woodland on a regular basis.

I can hear the scepticism of some readers bouncing back at me, so will give this a little more explanation. Within the average child spending 6.5 hours per day in front of a screen, projects like this are crucial in re-connecting children and young people with the outdoor environment in a safe and educational way.

Beyond this, it gives them opportunity to learn about the natural environment, how to handle risks, to use their own initiative to solve problems and cooperate with others. Whilst the focus is on emotional and social skills as well physical activity, a passion for the natural world and the skills learnt from Forest School lessons can have academic benefits in the sciences, literature, art, geography, music and design/technology. It is also more likely to inspire an interest in climate change issues and sustainable living later in life, problems which will require increasingly urgent solutions as today's children become adults.

This is a movement not just confined to well-funded private schools, but one which is slowly being rolled out and encouraged nationally for state schools too.

Unsurprisingly, this very much appealed to the barely-concealed hippy (and hipster) in me. This is something I would have loved as a child, as many of my happiest  memories of playing were outdoors and in the countryside. Even now, as an adult, I am happiest around a campfire or pottering in my vegetable patch and write mostly from the back garden wrapped up in a big blue coat.

So, on a drizzly Friday in May, I donned waterproofs and wellies to follow the teacher and 20 Year 2 children into the woods on the school's grounds. Teacher asked the what various trees and plants were along the way. I was astounded at their knowledge – I had no idea what a hawthorn tree looked like and was quickly proven to not be smarter than a six-year-old.

The children then had a lesson in whittling. Twigs quickly became wands, drum sticks, conductors' batons, ribbon wands and even quills after an English lesson about Samuel Pepys, all with the help of a vegetable peeler. One boy asked if being a whittler was a job as he was really enjoying the activity, I'm hoping they have inspired the school's first internationally renowned professional whittler. They then learnt how to lash sticks together to create photo frames and how to tie basic knots.

I had not worked closely with children before this placement and was surprised at how much I enjoyed it, especially as a Forest School teacher. It goes without saying that I found it really rewarding.

This is a job which ticked plenty of my boxes and whilst perhaps it isn't for me right now, it is certainly something I can see myself doing later in life. After all, you would spend your days in the woods, teaching happy children their favourite lesson. What's not to like?

INTERIOR DESIGNER

It is a sign that you have reached true adulthood when the idea of furniture shopping becomes genuinely exciting. Some of us have a better eye for it than others and some of us can make designing the interior of others' homes their full-time profession; this is what Rebecca Hadley does. Unsurprisingly, she has the most Instagramable flat I have ever seen, which is also something I have never said about a flat before. Most of us who are not gifted with the eye still know what good looks like when we see it; while our tastes might vary, we can usually feel the deeply satisfying *feng shui* of a beautifully balanced space.

Rebecca started working life as a buyer for major brands, including Selfridges and Urban Outfitters, and specialised in homewares and furniture as it combined her business head and with love of design. After ten years she decided to cut out the middleman and launch her own business, MakeMyHouseHome. com. MMHH will help with everything from full home renovations to one-off consultations, but specialises in creating furniture packages.

Of course, setting up your own business is not easy, and Rebecca laid out plenty of the challenges to me over tea when I first arrived. It's a very steep learning curve and it takes a lot of work to not get very far – initially things can move very slowly. There is no one there anymore to pat you on the back when you do well and help you figure out where you are going wrong, something you barely realise is there in the workplace, but that is actually quite appreciated. Working with others means you usually know when you are going in the right direction (or not), but when you are self-employed, you are left to figure it out for yourself.

For all that, it also means that you are the one in control and can trust in your own ideas. You can combine creativity and business problem solving and are constantly learning new skills.

I spent my time with Rebecca helping with social media platforms by organising and scheduling posts and I helped to leaflet the local area to promote her business. I then tagged along on her visit to a rug supplier's warehouse; I never before realised that I had such strong opinions on so many rugs. To be fair though, they were great rugs. I had always assumed that each high street shop sourced their products from a range of suppliers across the UK and from around the world. This rug supplier, however, worked with the majority of popular high street brands who all sourced directly from this one warehouse, and could choose products that fit their brand.

In between all of this, I asked Rebecca as many questions as I could about what it's like to be an interior designer and why she chose the career. She spoke about how she had always liked interiors; growing up, her parents were constantly re-designing and re-decorating each room of their house in one big cycle. When she moved into the industry professionally, she found she enjoyed it not so much because of the way she could make spaces look, but because of how it makes a client feel and taking pleasure in how beautiful items are made.

Interior design, for her, connects people and evokes emotion by creating a sanctuary space. She's able to give clients something they will enjoy every day for years, even decades to come.

In terms of what she does on a day-to-day basis, few days are the same. This is partly down to the project-based nature of client work but is also a major feature of running your own business. This means everything from website design, accounting, social media and arranging deliveries, to selecting the right tradespeople to work with and building relationships with suppliers. Behind the scenes, she also needs to analyse sales, research market trends and go to trade shows to meet wholesalers. For her clients, Rebecca is always running off to take measurements, collect samples, create mood boards and presenting and refining her ideas. Finally, there is overseeing the implementation of her designs; so everything that you would naturally expect to come with project management. Variety really is the spice of life to this career!

There were plenty of career attributes that matched up here, as interior design definitely covered my desire to have a creative career with elements of entrepreneurship. I loved that Rebecca was constantly on the move and didn't spend much time behind a desk. Problem solving and intellectual stimulation were certainly there, and she always needed to be able to come up with new ideas. Personal impact is there too as she is the main force for her business.

Much of it, though, comes down to having that eye for style and design. Looking at Rebecca's flat, it was all too obvious that she had that knack – to be brutally honest, I don't think I do. Comparing how she decorates her personal space to how I do mine, I am happy to stick my hand up and say I could never compete with her natural flare for this. I think my creative skills may be put to better use elsewhere.

LANDSCAPE GARDENER

If you were to stalk my Instagram, you may notice that there is more than one enthusiastic photo of homegrown, oversized courgettes; I quite like gardening. Given that the point of trying out so many different careers is to explore literally everything that I thought there was even a remote chance that I might like to do, seeing what life would be like if I spent it wholly in the garden was up next.

I spent a drizzly day working with Anthea Harrison, of Anthea Harrison Garden Design, in Stansted village. I had no idea that Stansted was anything other than an airport, but it turns out it's a beautifully quaint village on the Hertfordshire-Essex border, and you can't hear a single aeroplane.

The morning was spent in a client's garden, a large project that included extensive construction work, as it was being totally re-designed. It was very close to completion when I joined so I helped out with some of the planting, training some of the clematis' and titivating some of the bushier plants (note: innuendos in a professional setting are not encouraged, much to my disappointment). I pulled on my raincoat and got stuck in, taking pleasure in the physical nature of the work and the chance to get a bit muddy.

The level of botanical knowledge needed (and my total lack of any) quickly became apparent as Anthea and her colleague mixed the Latin for at least 20 different plant species into general conversation. I spent a fair amount of time pretending I knew exactly which plant they were talking about and nodding along when they started to go into details about the properties of each one. Once they had shown me which plant they were referring to, I realised that I knew most by sight, if not by name. In my garden, it would be known as 'that tall prickly pink one'. Anthea's extensive knowledge of botany was to be expected given her career choice, though I found the prospect of learning everything about the necessary 600 different species rather daunting.

As the rain went from drizzle to downpour, we headed back to Anthea's home-based office and she talked me through what it's like to be a garden designer in a bit more detail. Most start with a year's diploma at a horticultural college like Capel Manor and then start building their own businesses. The entrepreneurial side certainly appealed, as well as the more obvious outdoors-based, creative and innovative aspects.

We then discussed the design process, from initial consultation with a client, through to finished award-winning garden, explaining the computer aided design (CAD) programme she uses to design and create technical drawings of every aspect of a project. Anthea also talked me through how much went on in the background that the client was rarely aware of and how closely the garden designer works with other contractors, both from a design perspective as well as project management.

Garden designing is 'outdoor architecture'. After working with and interviewing Anthea, I saw how many separate and highly specialised skills a garden designer needs to get a job done, and any assumption that this is a 'housewife hobby career' would be totally misplaced.

I was surprised how many boxes of mine this career ticked, and by how intellectually challenging it was. Things like problem solving, creativity, innovation and non-desk-based work made sense, but the variety of project-based self-employment also brings variety and personally adding value.

The more I have thought about the 'making a difference' box for this career, the more I see how in some circumstances it could be included. Yes, you are providing a service for an almost exclusively luxury product, but on the other hand, you are spending your time creating something of living and bio-diverse beauty that clients will enjoy for decades to come. Anthea also highlighted the work she has done with the public sector to re-design public areas in town centres, showing an entirely different side to garden designing. Creating beautiful public spaces that contain plants rather than concrete can be used to encourage local communities to spend more time together and in nature. Green spaces have been proven to improve mental wellbeing and help to build sustainable communities.[51]

This is a career that I would never have seriously considered for a second if it weren't for trying out so many, let alone actually going out and seeing how it's done. It has challenged my assumptions and led me to a career that I think I would genuinely enjoy. Whilst I decided that it might not be a job for my 20s, I can certainly see myself retraining to do this in later life, such as when I have a family. Garden designing is a career that combines both the left and right sides of your brain – technical and creative – and best of all, it's outdoors!

TOUR GUIDE

On my trip through Venezuela, I had the chance to see if my dream of being paid to travel was as good as it sounds. I led the tour group for a couple of days and interviewed the leader, Kim Owen.

It's safe to say, whilst being a tour leader is pretty close to sounding like the best job in the world, it is also far more nuanced than that. Like any job, it is hard work and has its pros and cons.

Kim's story

Kim has been professionally working as a tour leader for a company called Oasis Overland for four years, after spending two years as a geologist following university.

Having always wanted to travel, especially to see East Africa, Kim saved up and bit the bullet, going on an overlanding trip from Nairobi to Cape Town. By the end of the tour, she had 'fallen in love with the whole thing' and sent a job application off to their head office. She spent the next two years working in Africa, including going from Cape Town to Harare, before being sent to loop around Central Asia, Iran and Turkey – where I first met her – and then to South America.

It all sounds rather glamorous. The cliché that every day is different could not be truer than it is for a Tour Leader, with a huge variety of working environments. She says that it often doesn't feel like work as it's so sociable – she usually becomes good friends with her customers – and she has a permanent tan. She loves the self-sufficiency of being an overlanding tour leader as it gives her the flexibility to improve the itinerary as the groups travels. I experienced this first-hand in Uzbekistan, when Kim decided that we should take a rather long and last-minute detour to the shore of what was the Aral

Sea. It was very much a once-in-a-lifetime chance to see something of monumental environmental significance.

When everything is running smoothly and all the passengers are happy, she says it feels more like a lifetime of travelling with friends. But then, you go to countries like Venezuela or Iran and it's all substantially more stressful, as she is responsible for making sure the trip is as safe as possible in places where things can be far from what your mum would call safe.

Kim was keen to stress that 'it's a harder job than it seems', tour leaders will work all day every day for months at a time. There is no leaving the office at five and no weekends. You continuously must try to meet your customers' needs and expectations, which can 'vary wildly'.

On an especially memorable occasion, a passenger who had their passport stolen whilst drunk woke Kim at two in the morning for help. She spent the next three hours 'making consular bookings, researching processes and necessary visas problems before trying to wake the now hungover individual at seven in the morning to go get a police report for them'.

She found it hard to not have a personal life; it's expected that she won't be able to be there for friends' birthdays and weddings now, or even be able to go for a drink after work with them. It is also certainly not a career that will make you rich, but on the flip side, it means everyone who does that job, does it 'for the love of it.' She adores being able to show people less touristy places, 'seeing their excitement' and 'experiencing it with them'.

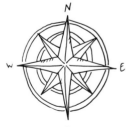

So what does she actually do?

The tour leader role is 'pretty broad'. Before a trip starts, there is a lot of planning, as Kim will get in touch with all of the local contacts and make bookings with them months in advance. This also means the itinerary must be planned down to the day – a challenge on a six-month trip across Africa, for example. There's a lot of budgeting and research involved too, to ensure the books are balanced and the group won't end up somewhere they shouldn't during Ramadan, for example.

When on the trip, it's about the logistics of getting passengers across a continent unscathed and happy, always being one step ahead so she can answer their many, many questions and generally making sure everything runs smoothly and to plan. Then there is the basics of organising meals and activities, cleaning, cooking, setting up camp and driving. With security issues, she and the driver will make a decision on the ground with information from local contacts in the area, and advised by head office. In Venezuela during some major protests, this meant changing the itinerary to avoid a certain area altogether and re-planning an entire section of the trip. Kim will also keep trip and driving notes, to pass onto the next tour leaders for the route; detailing exactly what time we left somewhere, how long it took to get to the destination and what we did along the way provides a reliable roadmap in incredibly remote areas of the world.

After the trip has finished, there is a fair amount of paper work and finalising the accounts, as well as often having to transit the truck to the starting point of the next trip or to a base where it can be stored. This can involve days more of driving. From Turkey to London or Cape Town to Cairo, for example.

What did I do?

Kim asked me if I would like to have a go at leading the group for a few days after we had crossed the border from Venezuela into the safety of Colombia, for a short excursion to Tayrona National Park, as she had to plan the next section of the trip in a nearby town. The national park is an area of beach-fronted area of dense jungle that can only be accessed by foot, with no phone signal or WiFi. My job was pretty simple – to get the group there and back, check them into accommodation and generally be as helpful as possible.

All did not go to plan. Actually, that's an understatement.

It was a complete car-crash.

The other members of the group had been travelling together for six months and were not so keen on the idea of the break from Kim's leadership being handed over to me. It was something I had not taken into consideration that I should have, and I very quickly learnt the lesson that you cannot lead those who do not wish to be led!

There is a difficulty in transitioning from friend to a leader who can understand and manage clients' expectations. I was reassured to learn that this is an issue that proper tour leaders can also face, when taking over from a group when the original leader flies home due to illness or a family emergency, for example.

My experience of tour leading, therefore, came mostly from shadowing Kim directly, rather than leading the group myself. This is something I regret, as whilst I got a very good insight into what's it's like to do Kim's job, it's not quite the same as doing it myself.

Being a tour leader would certainly fulfil a dream of being paid to travel and in the short-term, it's something I really could see myself doing. There would be absolutely no risk of getting bored in the mundane 9-5, I would constantly be experience new things and meeting new people. It would be a challenge, especially in the less 'safe' areas of the world that companies like Oasis Overland take passengers to. I found the problem-solving aspect and the direct impact I had on customer service rewarding. It is a hard job though, much harder than it first appears, and there are a lot of compromises that would need to be made.

On balance, I would need to find a way to combine it with something that is more of an intellectual challenge too, which is certainly not impossible. Hypothesising here, but maybe I could be a tour leader that is also a freelance political-travel-writer and journalist? Who knows!

INVESTIGATIVE JOURNALIST

Starting a new job on the day of an all-out tube strike across central London is not the most auspicious of beginnings.

I was joining the investigations team at The Telegraph, and it was my first exposure to the world of journalism and a national newspaper. This is the paper that exposed the MP expenses scandal and the Sam Allardyce case, among numerous others; I was incredibly lucky to have the opportunity to work with them, even if only for a week.

Journalism is an industry I hadn't seriously considered until I started this project as I didn't know if I was any good at writing. I had always assumed that I could make a positive difference with greater impact in other careers, rather than in journalism. What I didn't factor in is both that this is basically just wrong – exposing the MP expenses scandal has made a huge difference to parliamentary financial accountability, for example. I have also realised how much I enjoy writing since starting this project. I now know that I want that skill to be a predominant feature in whatever career I end up doing at the end of this journey.

In my naivety about the industry, however, I neglected to think through what the differences might be between reporting and working in Investigations specifically. Working as a reporter on the main news floor requires writing numerous stories each day, often to very tight deadlines on whatever topics are in the news that day.

Investigations, by its very nature, focuses on much longer-term projects and in-depth research. This is fantastic if you are working there for months or years. For a week, however, not so much. Because of the discrete nature of the work, I was also not able to shadow the people I was working with as, understandably, much of what they do doesn't really leave room for someone to tag along asking lots of questions.

This is the first time on my journey that it has been obvious that short-term work experience just isn't long enough to really get a sense of what it is like to work in this area. It was like trying to run before I understood anything about walking.

Whilst I learnt a huge amount with the Investigations team – we all really need to up our privacy settings, let's leave it at that – I realise now it is something that was simply too many steps ahead and in too short of a time frame. This is why there will be a Journalism Part Two career profile, which will hopefully be far more enlightening as it will focus on being a reporter.

TECH START UP

I pulled up outside a whitewashed stone cottage, nestled next to a stream in the heart of the Brecon Beacons, Wales. Not an obvious location for a tech start-up.

I was spending the week with Sort, an edu-tech (education technology) company that provide career advice, inspiration and a jobs board for 16-25-year-olds. Users enter details of the industries that they are interested in, their hobbies and things that they value in a career, such as creativity or leadership (sound familiar?!). The 'Sort Engine' algorithm will then suggest career types and job opportunities tailored to the individual. I came along to help whilst the platform was in its Beta testing, but the full launch was due a few months later.

Chris and Lucy, the founders of Sort, both have backgrounds as university lecturers and 18 months before had decided to risk going it alone as they felt that they could do more to help young people than what was on offer. They worked to find investors, develop a platform and create content, ready for testing by some rather unforgiving local sixth form students.

They got in touch with me a couple of months into my project and after a few Skype conversations, I began working as a freelance content writer for them. After all, careers advice is one thing I can write about! But it took a full eight months to arrive at their cottage front door for a formal work experience placement.

What did I do?

One thing I love about working in start-ups is the access to a wide variety of opportunity to build new skills and, by extension, how quickly you need to learn to pick those things up. This mental flexibility makes every day varied and a challenge.

I started by editing and uploading the 20 articles I had written for them over the past few months to the website. I then moved from the written word to developing more visual content for the platform by interviewing from behind the camera. Sort want to have as many interviews with people from a range of careers as possible, from musicians to NHS nurses. We very strongly agree on this point, as diverse careers education is something I advocate for.

I really enjoyed using film, as this is not something I do too much of, though it quickly became obvious that I needed more practice with the kit. One of the shoots with a local singer did not go to plan – I had not tested the microphone with my camera first, and out came a loud and constant buzz whenever I hit record. I had no spare camera or microphone.

On the marketing side, I sent out mailshots to existing subscribers and created animated drawings to explain and promote certain career paths – that was a new skill too. I went along to a handful of meetings to learn about how to pitch to the client companies Sort were trying to get on board, to build the number of job opportunities available.

Much of my time, however, was spent sitting in with Chris and Lucy brainstorming about business strategy and their plans for the future, which I found fascinating. It was great to be able to work on a project where I strongly identified with the vision and felt it could make a difference to young people's career decisions.

As with several of the placements I have worked in that are start-up based, I really enjoyed the camaraderie and creativity, the openness to new ideas and problem solving, as well as how every person in the company makes a significant impact. This creates a workplace that provides a real challenge, which is something that I'm really looking for.

Generally, international travel or outdoors work is not especially likely and much of the work is desk and office-based, though of course this is dependent on the start-up. This has been an issue that I have struggled to reconcile throughout my journey – how do I find a job that has the intellectual and creative challenges I'm looking for, but that also isn't entirely behind a computer screen? Whenever autumn starts to move into winter, it is something that I find myself thinking about more and more. For months of the year it is dark when I would get into work and dark when I would leave.

Working for an innovative tech start-up, especially one like Sort that matches my interest in careers education and so would come down heavily on the scales for all the brain-burning attributes I'm looking for, but it doesn't answer the question of how I can balance it with the great outdoors. I want a job that alleviates rather than encourages Seasonal Affective Disorder (SAD).

NEWS REPORTER

I have been back at The Telegraph, following my stint with the Investigations team. This time I was working as a news reporter, spending one week with Foreign News and then a week on the Education desk. There was also a smattering of security, defence, social media and trending news in there too, for good measure.

I'll say it up front – I think this might be the one.

One thing that I have learnt from this journey is how much I enjoyed the opportunity to write all the time, something I have not done as an adult. Journalism, of course, would allow me to do that on a daily basis and would even pay me (a somewhat questionable amount) to do so.

Working as a news reporter gave me far more insight into the life of an average journalist than the specialism of Investigations. It involves pretty much all of the things I enjoy doing beyond writing too; talking to interesting people, not sitting at a desk all day, the opportunity to analyse and question national and international events.

Unsurprisingly, I found a great deal of satisfaction seeing something I had written in print. I got a pretty large adrenaline kick out of the fast-paced nature of having to write to very short deadlines and I relished in the opportunity to write both daily news and more strategic opinion pieces.

The principle reason I originally started working for government was because I want to make a difference – partly as a way of giving back to a world where being born into a middle class London family meant I am automatically in its luckiest 1%. Partly, because I believe we all have a responsibility to live for more than ourselves, and I sense that much of career fulfilment for me will come down to this. This was the case when I was 22, and I see nothing wrong with being driven by optimistic ideals at age 24 too. Let cynicism follow in the decades to come.

Whilst I ended up growing frustrated at several aspects of working for government, journalism would be another way to make a difference. The media can provide a platform to challenge perceived ills in society – they (mostly) present the facts, rather than 'alternatives.'

I now wonder how it had not occurred to me before that being a foreign correspondent (still aiming for that travel) might actually be my dream job. It seems so obvious, like everything has clicked into place.

Journalism genuinely could tick all my boxes. There are question marks over innovation and problem solving though – the latter as I feel it is perhaps something that sits comes with seniority, the former, however, is a much bigger question.

The future of journalism

The industry faces perhaps its greatest challenge since its foundation – how to create a sustainable business model when so much news can be obtained for free online. Only a tiny proportion of us millennials pay for our news, and increasingly fewer members of older generations do either.

News organisations across the world are grappling with this issue and, as yet, there is no viable solution. There is now paid access to 'premium' content, such as with The Telegraph, or access to news only through fully paid subscriptions, such as with the Financial Times, but how long can these models last?

Media outlets are having to become increasingly digitally savvy and some businesses such as The Independent have abandoned print media altogether.

One consequence of this is shouldered by journalists themselves, as they need to work harder for decreasing wages in real terms and substantially less job security – redundancies can be rife.

Beyond this, as someone seriously considering entering the profession, I'm acutely aware that it is not a future-proofed option. Automated writing software has already begun writing sports news in several major news platforms.[52] After this stark realisation, I'm left asking if journalism is a sensible career option for the long-term.

This is a question I posed to many of my temporary colleagues and their answers did not comfort me, as both junior and senior reporters cautioned me against entering the profession. However, their passion for their jobs was consistently obvious – they all seemed to love what they do, it just kept coming back to sustainability and affording a semi-comfortable life. These aren't people spending money on pedicures and coconut water, they were just talking about things like rent and bills. It all sounded pretty bleak.

For some it no longer was a sustainable option; in the short time I was there, one was trying to get accepted to law school, another was looking into corporate communications and a third was applying for jobs in PR.

The challenge to this from other journalists was that the 'job for life' concept is dead. It is now common for people to retrain four or more times throughout their career, and this trend is increasing.[53]

Perhaps this is where portfolio careers should be pointed. Not putting all your eggs in one career basket, but instead spreading them out[54] could mean you benefit from still being able to do what you love, while ensuring your skillset remains broad and up-to-date.

Perhaps I could be a freelance foreign correspondent, tour guide and work part-time for an international development charity all at the same time?

CHAPTER FIVE

ON FINDING THE TIME AND THE MONEY

happiness depends upon ourselves.
– aristotle[+]

[+] Well, he sort of said it. That's what it got translated to a couple of millennia later, along with a little literary flourish. You get the point.

*T*hat's brave!
    Well, you have got balls.
I could never do that though.
It's not for the likes of me, too scary.

I am not brave. You can do it. It is for the likes of you. And I certainly do not have balls.

This is a conversation that I have had time and time again. Fear of major change and fear of the unknown are what puts most people off. At least staying where you are is safe; it's a known quantity. You might not like it very much, but there is a lower risk of total calamity. When you get into work every morning, you know what you are up against and you know what you need to get through. If you left, all of that would disappear. There would just be this infinite emptiness spreading out before you, nothingness. That can feel absolutely terrifying, gut-wrenchingly so. This dread can force us into the sort of inertia that keeps us in jobs we hate for years, a decade even; it's much easier to stay safe. This is the emotional blocker that needs to be overcome and by slowly networking and building up short-term placements – bit by bit it will become progressively less terrifying and more realistic. But what about more practical issues?

Practically, how do you go about getting from 'I hate my job' to 'this is my amazing new career and life'?

It's all very well and good to feel inspired by ideas or the story of someone else who has packed it all in, but how do you make it realistic for you; what about time and what about money?

Finding the time

We are all busy. We all struggle to find the time to behave like responsible, organised adults.

Adulting is hard and it can feel like we are only really pretending to do it, we are imposters in our own lives. Things like washing bedsheets and towels on, at least, a semi-regular basis doesn't always happen. We all know we should be making a packed lunch instead of spending exorbitant amounts on Pret, but yet when that Sunday evening comes around, the idea of making a week's worth of packed lunches feels like hell on earth. The shower curtain rail has been broken for nearly two months and realistically isn't going to get fixed any time soon. And we can't steal our flatmate's shampoo for much longer without being caught. We know we should have some savings by now and that they should be sensibly put in an ISA; we definitely don't have an ISA. Credit cards however, we definitely do have a few of those.

Life admin gets in the way of life, so we don't prioritise it.

Where, then, do we find the time for exploring other careers? It feels like we barely have enough time for the career we are currently in. Whilst we may be clockwatching between the hours of 9:00 to 5:00 during the day, and between 5:00 and 9:00 the next morning, we don't have a minute to spare.

Realistically, the vast majority of us simply cannot afford to quit our jobs and not earn anything for a few months while we ponce off to 'find ourselves'. What this chapter will talk you through is figuring out how to practically go about trying out other careers without being a millionaire. We will look at different approaches you can take that might involve a little bit more patience and a few financial compromises but are fundamentally do-able.

Lunchtimes, evenings and weekends

This is when you have your coffee meetings and go to networking events. Find little slivers of time to fit in around your normal working day without having to make substantial compromises. You can still make those leaving drinks or that friend's birthday dinner, you just might not get there until eight in the evening, instead of when you ordinarily would have. Perhaps you could take an hour and a half for lunch tomorrow and get in 15 minutes earlier and leave 15 minutes later that day to compensate.

Do you have the option to work from home one day each week in your current job? This cuts out an hour or two a day in commuting time, which could be spent doing all that emailing and organising of networking meetings.

Try dedicating an evening and a lunchtime every week to careers exploration, as if you were taking an evening class or had a hobby at that time. Monday lunchtimes and nights, for example, are booked out in your diary every week for the next three months, irrespective of whatever else you have on. Instead of having the Sunday night dread, you could be looking forward to spending the next day focusing on how to change your career instead. No one really does anything on a Monday anyway.

Annual leave

You really don't like your job. In fact, you would really like to never do it again. If you are currently working in a full-time, permanent job you will most likely be entitled to a minimum of 28 days paid holiday each year, if you include bank holidays.

Maybe this year, you don't use all of this for actual holidays, given that you want to leave your job anyway. Maybe this year you invest some of your annual leave in doing a few days' work experience or shadowing in three of four different industries that you're most interested in. It only needs to be a day or two in each if you are pressed for time. Yes, it will be pretty tiring to lose those few holiday days – they are precious – but this was never going to be easy. Please don't expect this to be easy.

An afternoon off

Consider if you might be able to go down to working four and a half days a week by taking one afternoon off each week. Is this something your organisation might allow? Could you afford the short-term drop in salary? Perhaps you could come to an agreement with to work compressed hours for a couple of months, if a salary drop isn't an option?

Having half a day off per week may not sound like much, but suddenly having five or six hours a week spare can make a significant difference. Over three months, that adds up to 12 half days, or six whole working days. These are days that you could put to trying other careers out and doing all the networking that you can.

Traditional sabbatical

This can be as radical or conservative as you want it to be. If you have been with your company for a while and feel you really need some time as far away from work as you can get, a proper mental break, then consider this option.

Unpaid leave for anything from a couple of weeks to three months could enable you to take a step back and when you find something you like, to step back completely by handing in your notice. This allows you to effectively test the water before formally committing to leaving your current job – you have the safety net of being able to go back if you absolutely have to.

Radical sabbatical

This is the option I went for – a career break or a gap year for professionals. I quit.

I did leave a few doors half-open though and kept in touch with plenty of people that I knew in my former industry, knowing that it wouldn't be too hard to go back again if I changed my mind. I made sure not to burn any bridges and was careful to ensure everyone knew that none of my decisions were personal to any of the colleagues I had worked with.

Which of these makes most sense for you?

These options are, of course, not mutually exclusive. You can combine a mixture of nearly all of them, depending on how intensely you are able to work on this each week – anything from one evening or lunchtime to quitting and concentrating on this full time.

Which of these makes most sense for you as a way to explore your career options?

Make a list for each one on what the pros and cons for you:

- Lunchtimes, evenings and weekends

- Annual leave

- An afternoon off each week

- Traditional sabbatical

- Radical sabbatical

Time is the most valuable commodity. It is intensely finite and yet ticks away eternally to remind us of that fact. You can't earn more of it, but you can invest it in intangible things like knowledge. Finding a new career is something you can invest time in. Yes, it's going to be hard and the last thing you might want to do is spend more time thinking about and doing work. This work-time is different, though, this can be exciting and the end result will make it more than worthwhile.

If you are in a position where you really can't stand day-to-day work life, that will likely impact how long you will be prepared to spend exploring other careers while still in your current job.

The more you hate your job, the less likely you are to spend months planning what you will do when you leave and the more likely you are to quit in a dramatic blaze of glory and just worry about the consequences later. If you are constantly bored, rather than experiencing full-blown blind, seething hatred, you are more likely to be able to tolerate it for another couple of months while you figure yourself out.

The one-step at a time approach

Whilst your end goal is to figure out exactly what it is you want to do for a living and to get an actual job in that area, there are an awful lot of steps in between there and where you are now. All of those unknown steps are rather intimidating. What helps, though, is breaking things down into much smaller chunks. Focusing on each step at a time, where only the next one is recognised and achievable, rather than searching immediately for your end goal, helps to put things in perspective.

You may only know what step one is right now – that is fine and is an achievement in itself. You don't need to worry about step two yet. If you were training to be a doctor, start with learning what all the body parts are called, don't worry about how to perform brain surgery yet.

Setting a rough deadline for when you intend to reach that final step will also help. It could be weeks, it could be months, or it could even be a year or two. This deadline needs to be realistic but still enough of a stretch to keep you motivated without getting complacent, though the further along the plan-job hate graph you are, the more motivated you are likely to feel, and the shorter your deadline is likely to be. If you are the sort of person who needs a little bit of pressure, put weekly reminders in your calendar, counting down how many weeks to go until your deadline.

Each time you have completed a step, then figure out what your next step is and write it down. Putting pen to paper (or at least fingers to keys) and then sticking it somewhere noticeable commits you to following through far more than if you are simply keeping it in the back of your head. Step one could simply be finishing reading this book and figuring out a few jobs to try. Steps two through six could be shadowing someone in five different jobs, each for a day. As you get going you will begin to think through what you do and don't like, further clarifying your understanding of yourself. Each step will get easier until you eventually figure out your solution.

Ambiguity and uncertainty are often unnerving as we are always expected to have a plan. We are constantly being asked what our next move is, where we want to be in five years' time, what do we want to have done by our next milestone birthday. This means that the concept of having absolutely no answers to any of these types of questions isn't something we are often faced with. Even more alien is the idea of being happy about not having any answers.

Embrace that uncertainty; it leaves so much room for unexpected opportunity.

Like everyone else, I am constantly asked what I'm planning next, where I want to be and so on. These days, my answer is that I don't have a plan. I don't have a set-in-stone goal that I am aiming to reach. I'm just figuring it out as I go along. This time two years ago, I would have found that a horrendous answer and it would have stressed me out. Today though, I leave all my doors open. Sometimes, by aiming for a goal with such certainty, we are blinded to other opportunities that are right in front of us; often these are opportunities that we never could have envisaged for ourselves. But yet, here they are. They can end up taking you down a path you didn't see coming, and surprisingly often, the unexpected turns out to be just what we were looking for all along, we just didn't know it at the time.

This idea of taking things one step at a time and of using lunchtimes and evenings or taking small chunks of time off work to explore your career options also stands true for when you do eventually find your 'thing'.

Balancing careers

Let's say you have decided that you would like to design jewellery and sell it on Etsy. You don't necessarily have to immediately leave your accountancy job just because you have figured it all out. You could decide to take a more risk adverse path by slowly building up one career option while reducing the other. You might start designing and creating your jewellery in your lunchtimes, evenings and weekends. After a few months, you could switch to working compressed hours or four days per week. After giving that a go and proving your concept by managing to successfully start selling your pieces online, you could try taking a traditional sabbatical to see if you could get your business truly off the ground.

CURRENT CAREER   NEW CAREER

This is where you are at now. Five days a week you are in your current career and at no point are you trying out anything new.

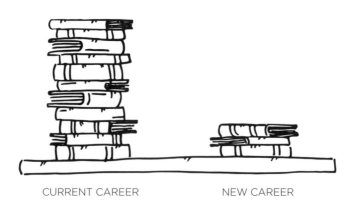

CURRENT CAREER   NEW CAREER

Using small slices of spare time on your weekends, during the evenings or even on your commute, you slowly start exploring the new career you are considering pursuing, while still working in your old one.

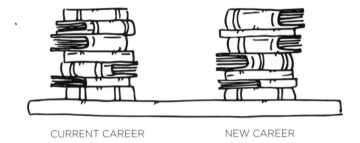

CURRENT CAREER   NEW CAREER

Over time, you increase the hours you put into your new career and reduce those into your old one.

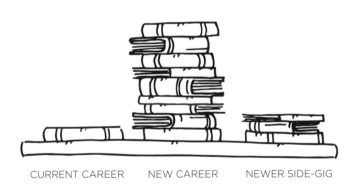

CURRENT CAREER   NEW CAREER   NEWER SIDE-GIG

Finally, your new career becomes your main source of income and occupies most of your time. You might also choose to do a little something else on the side too that you discovered is of interest whilst making your switch.

How to handle the money

In the world of work, time and money is often the same thing. How you spend your time determines your income and so the suggestions that have been made on how to use your time to explore other careers will at some point start to impact your finances in most probably a negative way. Depending on the salary of the career that you are planning on leaving, this could be a rather large issue to say the least and could easily prevent you from taking the plunge in the first place.

If you are planning on spending some time focusing on what exactly it is you want to do for a living, the chances are things could get a bit tight financially through that transition period. Where is that money going to come from? If you are earning enough now to be able to save a small amount each month and already have some savings put aside that you can draw on, then great. But what if you don't? Compromises will need to be made and you will need to start planning so that you have time to build up to the amount you need.

Often, we quite simply don't have anything left at the end of each month, or if we do have a little, it usually goes towards saving for that elusive house deposit. All of this means that we aren't able to justify spending money on career choices (we have already established that we are quite happy to spend plenty on our dating lives though – priorities).

We are advised to aim for a high salary and/or we are advised to follow our (usually badly paid) dreams. We are left rolling our eyes and feeling like we need to choose between a decent wage and following our passions; these almost always seem to be mutually exclusive. I will tell you to follow your dreams and I will tell you that money is important. It is unquestionably and undeniably important. We have to earn a living – there is a baseline minimum that we all need on a day-to-day basis and it is unrealistic to pretend otherwise. But, how much is that figure for you? What is the minimum that you are prepared to earn to do the things you love? And how do you make doing the things you love pay properly? There is always the outside chance that you will fall in love with investment banking and corporate law, in which case you are one of the lucky ones as you won't ever need to worry about your finances again, but let's face it, that's not massively likely. Most of those dream jobs – those long held passions – pay terribly. Hell, writing this book won't even cover four months' rent.

For many of us, we aren't even sure what those passions really are because we have never had the chance to properly test them out – money has almost always been part of the reason. To explore these things, at some point there will be a time where our finances will take a bit of a hit.

How much of a hit can you afford to take? Is there any fat you could trim, so you can start saving for that hit now? Given that what we choose to do with our time is how we earn our money, let's start with why you absolutely can justify spending time and therefore money on career development, and why this absolutely should be prioritised.

Can money buy happiness?

When we talk about happiness in relation to our earning power, we can tie ourselves in knots. The consensus on if money can buy happiness, though, is a predictable no. As income rises you become used to the finer things in life so instead of becoming happier, you increasingly compare yourself with your peers. You are left always wanting more which obviously isn't great for your happiness levels.

This is so well-documented that it has its own academic concept, the Easterlin paradox; economists have found that there is no correlation between higher salaries and an improvement in happiness. If you live in a wealthier country and have a higher salary, it is more likely to make you unhappy.[55][56]

Essentially, if you are currently doing it for the money, the evidence shows us that it's just not worth it for your happiness. City slickers who promise that they are just going to 'do it for ten years to earn the money, then I'll quit', invariably do not quit. Sound familiar?

Once you start earning big money it becomes addictive, making it much harder to walk away from. No one wants to switch from Waitrose to Lidl; it just becomes harder and harder to break away from a certain lifestyle, even when it's your happiness at stake.

Conversely, happier people have been proven to earn more because happiness substantially improves productivity and likeability; it can improve productivity by 12%.[57] That's not necessarily to say that these are people made happier by office perks, even if they are more satisfied by them; this rise in productivity is driven more by people with a personal disposition toward happiness.[58] A genuine and deep sense of personal contentment, rather than happiness through appeasement; CEOs take note, bean bags don't cut it. Some economists argue that if enough people are happy in their work, the impact on productivity could be a factor in strengthening an economy as a whole.[59] All the more reason to make sure you love your career choice.

Happy people, it seems, earn more but earning more does not bring happiness.

What should we do about that statement then? By spending time focusing on your career choices and making a career change, you will earn more in the long run as you will be more likely to be happier in your career, even if it takes a short term financial hit to get there. So, don't stress about losing (or never having) the big bucks. Yes, you need to earn enough to live in a certain level of comfort and security but focus on the difference between need and want. You can define what 'certain level of comfort' means for you but bear in mind that all those wants won't get you very far in improving your happiness.

Needs vs. wants

What we need to do is mix some idealism with a healthy dose of realism: figure out the absolute basic minimum income that you need.

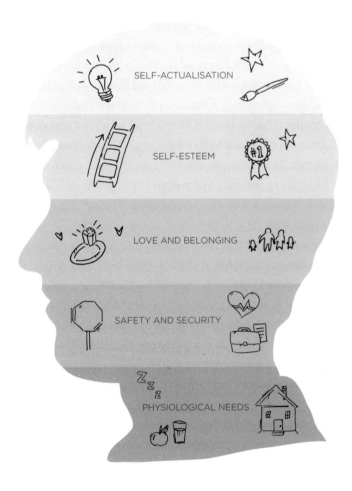

Maslow's Hierarchy of Needs

To work this out, let's start with figuring out what's important. Take Maslow's Hierarchy of Needs as a guide, a well-known and often used explanation for human need.[60] This can help you clarify what are your needs and what are your wants. There are five levels, starting with the absolute biological essentials to life: oxygen, food, water, shelter and so on. Then, it progresses upward to include things like safety and security through law, order and freedom from fear (not living in a warzone or failing state). The third is about personal connections and intimacy of relationships with those around you, as well as belonging to a group (through family, friends, work, hobbies, and so on). Then comes the slightly more abstract fourth level, of self-esteem and respect gained from others, which includes the need for individuality and independence. The highest level is self-actualisation, which includes things like finding meaning and purpose in your life, fulfilment and feeling that you can reach your full potential – something which many of us struggle with.

Maslow originally said that you needed to complete one level before you can be motivated by the next; you can't achieve level five without fully completing levels one to four. He later changed his mind, realising that it is not 'all-or-nothing' in each level, merely a 'more or less' scenario.[61] Take the property market in the South East England as an example: many millennials will struggle to own their own home. This should have minimal impact on their sense of connection with others, achieving success in their work or hobbies or plenty of the other factors.

Employment is an especially pertinent example of this. You do not have to be currently employed to access the higher of Maslow's levels, you only need access to a stable labour market so that, if absolutely necessary, you know that you could get some form of job to sustain yourself. Knowing this can give you the freedom to explore your options and search for meaning and purpose while not in full-time employment – just ask any 18-year-old on a gap year, or perhaps someone who is taking a somewhat radical sabbatical.

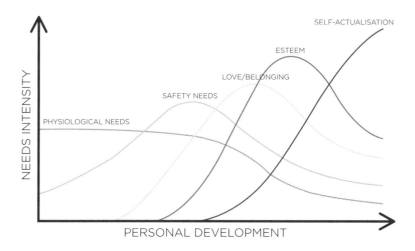

Dynamic Hierarchy of Needs

So maybe a hierarchy of needs isn't quite accurate in reflecting the complexity of our lives. This dynamic hierarchy of needs is perhaps more apt. It shows that there is a high degree of overlap between the levels, and most importantly that the highest level, self-actualisation, becomes intensely necessary as the lower needs are fulfilled.

So, what is the point of all of this?

What the Maslow chart highlights are your needs – things that are integral to your wellbeing and happiness. Your needs should absolutely include self-development and a search for purpose and meaning in your professional (and personal) life. This can be factored in when you are figuring out the salary you need compared with the salary you have now or the salary you want; you have permission. This also means you can afford yourself the justification of the opportunity-cost that taking some time off or away from your current job to focus on this.

I started aggressively saving as much of my salary as I could in the months leading up to my sabbatical project so that I had a small amount of savings to fall back on during what I knew would be leaner times financially. I drank significantly less alcohol. I asked friends over to mine and to meet at their flats, rather than meet them at restaurants, pubs or bars. I stopped buying new clothes altogether. I took the bus instead of the train wherever possible. I also started to look around for 'side-gig' type jobs that meant that I could earn a little extra during hours that worked for me. Essentially, I went back to living with shoestring student budget mentality, but whilst I was still earning a permanent salary.

Bear in mind that any compromises you will make will be for a short and defined period of time rather than for the long term. So, whilst your social life may take a bit of a hit for a few months, it is just for a few months and it will be worth it. You've got this.

Let's start by assessing your current income and expenditure.

Current income

What is your current monthly income after all taxes, student loans, credit card loans and other non-negotiable deductions? Create a table with two columns. There should be your expenses in one column – rent/mortgage, bills, food shopping, transport, social life, clothes, toiletries, beauty, subscriptions, and anything else – and a second column with how much you spend on each per month. At the bottom, list your overall expenditure for that month and next to that how much you can save.

Savings suggestions

- Are there any clothes or gadgets that you could sell?
- If you belong to a gym, could you downgrade your membership to a cheaper option or stick to running outdoors for a bit?
- When you do go out, live by Groupon deals and dining club discount cards like the Tastecard. Sign up for things like Meerkat Movies instead of paying full price for cinema tickets.
- Delete Deliveroo and Uber (or switch to occasionally working for them).
- Make your own packed lunches for work. Every. Single. Day.
- Maybe you could pull out of that mates holiday this year?
- Switch to shaving and painting your own nails over a wax and Shellac.
- Go through all your direct debits and see if there are any that you could pause for a few months. If you are using Spotify, Netflix, Amazon Prime, Audible and a monthly coffee subscription box, for example, is there any room to cut a few of them temporarily?
- Look at your utilities suppliers – are there any savings that could be made by switching? Use comparison websites as well as websites for advice like moneysavingexpert.com.
- The same goes for your phone contract; could you switch to a SIM only deal for £10 per month instead of £30-40 for a contract.
- Download savings apps and link them to your current account. Some round up your spending to the nearest pound so help you save without really noticing, others analyse your spending and advise on where you can make savings. Have a look at Moneybox, Chip and Squirrel, though there are plenty of others available.

- Explore budgeting apps and current accounts like Monzo, to help you be more aware of your spending and improve budgeting.

- Can you put everything you save into a high interest bank account, or one that will give you a cashback sum when you switch to them? Do your research: there are plenty of deals to be had with this.

- Would you be able to take on a side-gig? A few hours a week doing things like tutoring, market research, TV & film extra work, managing the social media for a small business, babysitting and proofreading will all make a substantial difference over the space of a few months.

- Could you consider something more drastic like move to a flat with a cheaper rent for a year, or even back in with your parents or relatives if that's an option?

Generally speaking, some of this is easier to do in the spring and summer than it is in the depths of winter; it is easier to meet friends in parks, arrange picnics and have BBQs at home rather than always going out to pubs, bars and restaurants. You can more easily swap a gym membership in for outdoors exercise in better weather, as well as having less of a need to hunker down for a Netflix binge. You will use substantially less heating, electricity and gas in the summer, so your utilities bills should be cheaper. Obviously, this isn't to say it can't be done in the winter, just that everything in life is a little easier when you are actually getting your daily dose of Vitamin D.

Many of these things are life's little luxuries that keep us going when we are miserable and so are frustrating to think of giving up, but they all add up. Remember, though, that you are aiming for a life where you don't rely so heavily on these little things to get you through the week. You won't necessarily feel quite so much of a need to make each day a little bit better by doing them, because each day will already just be a good day. When you have made the changes you want to in your life, you can always start them back up again. Short-term financial pain, long-term life fulfilment gain.

Draw a chart to assess your current spending – what fits into the 'wants' category and what fits into the 'needs'?

Where can you afford to make some savings? Be as brutally honest as you can be with yourself.

Roughly estimate how much you can realistically save per month, incorporating only your financial needs, combined with the ideas suggested over the past couple of pages.

On starting placements

You have done lots of networking; you have carved out a little bit of time; you have figured out what it is you think you are looking for from a job; you have figured out how you will save up a little money. You might have even finally found and organised a placement, and it is the morning of day one. What do you do now? What should your goals be?

This should be a very different experience to the one you had in Year 10, it is not the compulsory work experience that you did as a 14-year-old – you are here out of choice and this specific placement at this specific time is an intentional and well-orchestrated decision; it is an opportunity you have created.

It is also unlikely to be a paid internship, so whilst there might be a small amount of work for you to do, the emphasis should be more heavily weighted towards shadowing and asking questions of your new temporary colleagues. With an internship, the goal is usually a job with the company you will be working with. For this professional-level work experience placement, the goal is different; this is about you figuring out if this might be the right industry for you, rather than a specific job within this specific company. You don't need to come to any firm decisions, it's more to be able to say, 'yes this is something I want to pursue further', or 'actually maybe this isn't for me'. It just needs to be a pencil tick or cross, not necessarily one in permanent marker.

After asking as many questions as I could of the person I was shadowing and had done any work I had been tasked, I asked if they could introduce me to their wider team and talk me through everyone's jobs, before arranging coffees with colleagues whose roles I was particularly interested in. I would use the questions laid out in Chapter Four as a base for these conversations. As with previous networking meetings, asking about the bad as well as the good was invaluable. If I found something especially interesting and wanted to get a little more insight, I asked if there was any work I could do to help that person while I was there and if there was anyone else that they might be able to introduce me to so that I could find out more about a certain area. Remember the golden rules of networking.

Asking about working environment and culture was a big part of this process too – getting a range of different perspectives helped to get a more holistic understanding of what it was really like to work there on a day-to-day basis. Hearing about all the possible entry paths into the industry and the different types of jobs within it was also an incredibly helpful way to understand what my career could look like in a year, or five years from now, and allowed me to tap into a vital unwritten resource.

Mentoring

Along the way, you will meet a wide range of people from diverse backgrounds that you would have been unlikely to meet otherwise, and they will be doing jobs you may never previously knew existed. Like in any social situation, there will occasionally be someone that you immediately click with, who will naturally take particular professional interest in you and might be convinced to go above and beyond to help you reach your goals. Whenever you do meet these career heroes, don't let them go. Foster and prioritise these relationships, after a while they will transform from the occasional coffee to a formal or informal mentoring relationship.

Having a mentor has been proven to make a substantial impact on success, with mentees benefiting from faster rates of career progression, higher salaries, increased productivity, better networking skills and higher self-esteems, confidence and a better work/life balance.[62] A mentor will provide support and guidance by asking you questions, challenging you, helping you to set goals, advising you and giving you feedback. They might signpost you to certain resources or even facilitate introductions for you within their networks. This is someone who will fight your corner and guides you to making your own decisions on your journey. Most often, mentors are altruistic souls who are purely in it to give back and pass on knowledge. There is huge satisfaction in helping another person to develop and foster their talent.

These relationships can be formal to the extent of having an established working relationship with timescales and objectives. In this case, you would ask the person to mentor you after establishing a rapport with them over a period of weeks or months after initially meeting them. At the other end of the spectrum, they can be so informal that the word mentor is never even used; it could just be someone that you go for a drink or coffee with every couple of months and can bounce ideas off. This is up to you and your mentor to define and develop; it's about whatever works for you.

An alternative way of pitching a mentoring relationship is as being mutually beneficial through a relatively new concept – a reverse mentorship[63]. This is where a younger person mentors a professional from an older age group in all things millennial: social media, new technology and workplace trends, for example. This could also include brainstorming, where the more senior mentee talks through problems they are experiencing and you provide a 'millennial' approach and perspective on how you would solve the problem. In exchange, they mentor you on achieving your career goals within that career. This creates a very fluid mentor-mentee relationship, recognising that both partners have something to learn from each other rather than it always being one-directional. If you are still searching for a unique selling point (USP) that you can offer to a business in exchange for taking you on for work experience, then perhaps this is an idea you could further develop in a way that works for you.

From a more strategic perspective, initiatives like this present an opportunity to start breaking down some of the barriers and tensions we are experiencing with millennials in the workplace. It is opening up lines of communication that, until very recently, remained very firmly closed; strict hierarchies within the world of work are slowly beginning to break down into flatter structures from which we all stand to benefit.

If you haven't met anyone along the way that you feel would be right as a mentor, there are plenty of companies and charities that provide both paid and free career mentoring. Research what is available in your area and for your demographic. There are plenty of opportunities for free mentoring available for young people and those from disadvantaged backgrounds in the UK such as through The Prince's Trust.

During my time in doing so many different placements, there were many people that I came across who acted as informal mentors – some of them still do. There was one individual though, who really went out of their way to advise and support me through the project and who helped me organise further placements with the Police and in International Security, after I worked with them in Crisis Management. Having someone to look out for you professionally makes all the difference in keeping you on track and motivated, especially when making a somewhat daunting major career change.

Points for consideration

- I am not brave. You can do it. It is for the likes of you.
- Short-term financial pain, long-term life fulfilment gain.
- Find little slivers of time to fit in around your normal working day.
- Don't expect this to be easy.
- Time is the most valuable commodity. You can't earn more of it, but you can invest it in intangible things like knowledge.
- Break down the intimidating steps into much smaller chunks.
- Embrace uncertainty; it leaves so much room for unexpected opportunity.
- Compromises will need to be made. You will need to plan to build up to the amount of money you need.
- Happier people earn more because happiness substantially improves productivity and likeability.
- Having a mentor makes a substantial impact on success.

Questions to reflect on

- Do you have the option to work from home one day each week in your current job?
- Could you go down to working four and a half days a week by taking one afternoon off each week?
- Could you take a sabbatical to test the water?
- What is the minimum that you are prepared to earn to do the things you love?
- How much of a hit can you afford to take? Is there any fat you could trim, so you can start saving for that hit now?
- How could you reduce your current expenditure to help build up some savings?
- Who could you ask to be your mentor?

PROPERTY DEVELOPMENT

London Lofts head office is tucked away in a gated mews in a very trendy part of North London. I spent two weeks with the start-up, who specialise in unusual living spaces, and completely surprised myself with how much I enjoyed it.

I will admit up front that working in the property industry was a bit of a long shot. It was one of my more sensible sounding choices of the 25 careers and was something I was considering more because I had family members who worked in the industry that had peaked my curiosity over the years. However, what I found during my time with London Lofts was far more than a passing interest; it was my first taste of working somewhere with such an entrepreneurial spirit and such genuine camaraderie.

Whilst at university, I was set on working somewhere that didn't generate profit and was set against working anywhere without a specific social impact or benefit, which I had assumed ruled out the entire private sector; an assumption I made as a teenager with little real-world experience. What I realised pretty quickly on graduating though is that, yet again, my assumption was totally wrong – profit and positive social impact are by no means mutually exclusive and both can absolutely occur in the private sector.

The idea of working for a start-up was now especially attractive, as I imagined it would provide the greatest contrast possible to the 440,000-strong organisation I had recently left.

London Lofts sells and rents 'alternative' properties and, as their name suggests, it usually involves lofts, and some pretty nice ones at that. The sorts of places that most of us will only ever dream of owning. They also renovate unique properties and when

I was there, they were working on converting a disused chapel in Peckham that had once belonged to a 'banker-turned-bohemian who realised he was more of a banker after all'. I was incredibly fortunate that I arrived at (what I viewed as) the best part – the furnishing of the show house. I was given the dimensions of the rooms, the company credit cards and directed towards Ikea. This was probably the best task I was given to do in any of the 25 jobs. Free reign!

Much of the rest of my time with London Lofts was spent working on their social media, writing PR pieces, going all over London to look at properties, and taking part in general business brainstorming sessions.

On the importance of banter

London Lofts has three members of staff – two co-founders and a new recruit in his 20s. Between them, there is an awful lot of banter, bad singing and lunches at the local cafe. But those are the exact reasons why they seemed to work together so well. On several days, 40% of the time I spent with them was purely about bouncing ideas off each other, or to put it in long-abandoned office-speak, 'determining the strategic direction' of the company. We moved between that and the minutia of a sales deal without pausing for breath. And if someone had a good idea, 'great, let's go for it!' It sometimes felt impulsive, yes, but that's not always a bad thing.

Reflecting on my time there, the importance of getting on with your colleagues was never more apparent. This is something that seems obvious and that, of course, everyone would like. But I have never felt the real impact of working in such a friendly and happy environment. This is not to say my previous experiences with colleagues have been unhappy by any means, but never before on a Sunday evening had I looked forward to a Monday morning. Was it because I enjoyed what I was doing or because I enjoyed the company of the people? I can now understand why this distinction might not matter too much to many.

Recruiting 'people with personality' mattered to the chaps at London Lofts. It makes work feel less like work. Add the excitement of a start-up to the mix and you have an engaging, dynamic and creative workplace.

They even played Christmas songs – in November. Controversial.

I thoroughly enjoyed my time with London Lofts and got a huge amount out of the experience. I now know that at some point I want to work for (or launch my own) start-up as I loved the freedom, camaraderie and challenge that it can provide, along with that undefined entrepreneurial spirit.

I loved the problem-solving nature of working with the company, and found it intellectually stimulating in a different sort of way to what I had experienced before. Working in such a small start-up like London Lofts would certainly allow me to add a huge amount of value, be innovative and creative. Getting out of the office to look at prospective new properties or to give a viewing meant that every day was a bit different and varied, albeit I'm not sure if it would be varied, though perhaps the novelty would wear off over time.

I definitely want to explore working in the property industry further. However, I wonder if it would perhaps be better suited to an Emma in her 40s. The opportunity to work abroad and to travel through work is important to me in my 20s, as is the ability to make a difference and influence at a more strategic level. If I chose to pursue a career in property now, these elements would likely not come until later life, whereas working in other industries would provide me with those opportunities earlier.

Although if there was a way to build it into a portfolio career sooner, who knows!

INTERNATIONAL SECURITY

It takes a special kind of person to voluntarily spend a week in the rainy woods of England in the middle of winter. Fortunately, that is exactly the sort of thing I enjoy doing.

What has this to do with International Security, I hear you ask?

I spent a week with a small company that run crisis simulation exercises to train government officials and journalists for deployment overseas in hostile and disaster environments.

Their offices are based on an estate in the middle the Sussex countryside. As I arrived on a sunny morning driving past deer and horses to reach their converted barn, I couldn't believe that it was possible to work somewhere so green and open, and yet to be working at the cutting edge of security training so close to London. It is very important to me to have some of my working time spent outdoors, and I would certainly be able to do that here.

I spent the day helping to set up the crisis simulation – i.e. putting up tents – and learning more about the business. But, of course, the most interesting part was the exercise itself.

The consultancy was working to train diplomats who would be sent abroad at very short-notice to a crisis that involved British Nationals. This could include plane crashes, natural disasters or terror attacks, or even assisting the departure of Brits who are in a country experiencing a rapidly disintegrating security situation – think of any current conflict just before it became a full-blown conflict. Much of what these diplomats will do is to provide consular and logistical support, as well as on-the-ground picture of the situation for the government back in London. This puts people in situations that are understandably incredibly intense, pressurised and stressful, and at times decisions really could be life or death.

Ensuring these people have the appropriate training is crucial.

The crisis simulation

The teams undergoing training were put into a fully immersive and incredibly realistic scenario that mirrors actual events this one was to mimic an airplane crash where Brits were on board in an unstable country.

Actors are used to play the roles of British Nationals and 'locals' that are caught up in the situation. Several would be severely wounded, some unable to find relatives or partners, whereas others may play helpful – or unhelpful – local authorities. In more extreme training courses, some actors could even be 'abducted' or 'arrested' by hostile groups, so that participants can learn how to deal with hostage-type situations.

From my side, I was both an actor and helped out operationally behind-the-scenes. I was given the peculiarly morbid task of filling body bags to make them look somewhat realistic, as well as scattering debris around a nearby lake to make it resemble the aftermath of a plane crash.

I also shared the responsibility of manning the fictional country's national switchboard and directing stressed trainee's calls to various imaginary hospitals, morgues, embassies and government ministries. One lesson for me was that there are only so many ways I can change my voice to make it almost sound like I'm a different person – I am not a natural. The American ambassador should certainly not sound the same as a Russian doctor in a nearby field hospital, and neither of these should sound the same as the switchboard operator.

More practically, I also played the part of acting as a foreign journalist. My role was to hound each of the teams undergoing training with questions that I demanded needed answering that instant. I was also there to test participants' responses when I tried to photograph them, their work and operations, and the British Nationals under their care.

The wide contrast between each teams handling of the press showed just how important positive media relations are in a crisis. Ultimately, how events such as terror attacks are perceived back home, can be dependent more on press reporting than government's response – reputational awareness is something which, in reality, must always be kept in mind even when horrific events are unfolding right in front of you.

Finally, I acted out the part of a cleaner. Either that, or it was a sneaky way to get me to do some actual cleaning. All I'll say is that it gave me a renewed healthy respect for people who work in facilities management and services industries.

This is a job that I could never have known existed if it wasn't for this year. It is so bizarrely niche that even if I'd had the best careers advisor in the world at university, I would still probably never have discovered it. It certainly ticked an awful lot of my boxes, having one of the best mix of practical outdoors non-desk-based work, which was highly intellectual, all about innovative and creative problem solving and had plenty of strategic thinking. It was also incredibly varied and would make a tangible difference. Travel too would be an option. All in all, this is definitely one to think very seriously about.

CRISIS MANAGEMENT

When the first thing someone asks you on starting a new job is 'we want to know what you think', it's a pretty good indication of the type of organisation you have just joined. This is what I was asked on joining the Crisis Team at the British Council, the UK's international organisation for cultural relations and educational opportunities. It instantly made me feel empowered and trusted – two of the core features that I think contribute to career fulfilment.

The Crisis Team provide global on-call incident advice and support to British Council employees. They are there for any situation – from the detention of members of staff, to natural disasters or terror attacks. They also deliver training to in-county staff around the world to prepare them for how to respond to a crisis or incident. This is done by providing steps to follow, discussing how to gather and assess information, detailing who to contact in a crisis and so on, as well as by running simulation exercises to allow teams' space to practice their responses.

This is one of the few careers that I've tried where I've had some actual experience; I briefly worked at the Foreign and Commonwealth Office in the Libya Team in 2014, just as the country descended into near-civil war. I was also in the Department for Health, where I worked on crisis planning and response in Adult Social Care. This meant doing scenario planning for what to do if hundreds of care homes flooded or were without power, or if there was a junior doctor strike, for example. There were aspects of these roles that I'd really enjoyed, so I specifically wanted to do a placement in Crisis Management as one of the 25, to gain a better understanding of what a career in this field would involve, especially in an organisation that is so internationally focused.

On the importance of culture

The real standout of working with the Crisis Team was the people themselves – I have never felt so welcomed into a team before, including in previous permanent jobs. I found this to be the case across the entire British Council, everyone I spoke to happened to be more than willing to take the time to meet me for a coffee and give some career advice or help me with a project I had been working on. Other staff members repeated the sentiment to me time and time again – many truly felt that theirs was an organisation that was a sincerely friendly and open place to work. There was a noticeably flat structure, with senior staff being very approachable; the CEO's door seemed to be always open.

Things like this make a difference to how you feel about a job. You could have the most exciting role, but if red tape and unhelpful and unfriendly colleagues constantly hold you up, where day-to-day life is a battle of office politics, you are far less likely to want to go to work that morning.

The London attack

On my third day with the team, there was a terror attack in London at the Palace of Westminster and on Westminster Bridge, only a few hundred meters from the British Council's headquarters. The situation was horrendous; it left me feeling helpless, sick and livid.

Within 20 minutes, the Incident Management Team had met and had started gathering information, assessing the situation and deciding on a course of action. As it became clear that the attack was localised and did not directly affect the British Council site, the team decided not to lock down the British Council offices. Within 80 minutes of the attack, an email notification was sent to all London staff to provide reassurance and advice. This was followed by an email to all UK-based staff.

The impact of the attack on the British Council was low, but this is not always the case. As they operate in nearly 120 countries around the world, staff members are impacted whenever there is anything from civil unrest to outright civil war in a country, with various levels of response required, up to full-scale immediate evacuations.

That there are an awful lot of ticks in boxes from this placement, and it has the added bonus of actually using my MA degree, was satisfying. There would be plenty of travel involved to regions that I would love to learn more about. There would certainly be the opportunity to think strategically, as horizon scanning and geopolitical analysis would be essential. Things like problem solving, intellectual challenge and variety are fairly self-explanatory – this is certainly a job where I had never feel disinterested or fatigued! Ultimately, working in crisis management will directly help others, and personal decision-making can have a huge impact. Add to this the work that the wider British Council does in International Development and for soft power, it means elements like making a difference and personally adding value are major features of working here. The only areas I have questions over are that the vast majority of the work is desk-based, whether that's in the UK or abroad, and that creativity would be corporate-focused. Despite this, I felt that the positives of gelling so well with the team and the positive company culture tipped the scales firmly Crisis Management's favour, especially at the British Council.

In short, if they were to offer me a job, what would I say? Very probably, yes.

POLICE DOGS AND HORSES

Getting to spend your working day with dogs – right from the start that sounds like a winner of a career choice. I spent a few days working with one of the Metropolitan Police's Dog Support Units and, frankly, it was fantastic.

Monday morning, though, and I was well and truly lost somewhere in a muddy South London park with five minutes until I was meant to be reporting to a police station – not something you want to be late for. Frantically power walking, guided by a version of Google Maps that was out to get me, I staggered in six minutes late, dripping with sweat and with mud covering my slightly too high heeled ankle boots. At least if you are starting at rock bottom, it can only get better, right?

I was taken pity upon by Sarah, a Metropolitan Police Officer from the Met's Dog Support Unit and was invited to spend the day with her and her dog on their patrol rounds. First though, I needed to get kitted up. This involved a bullet-proof vest sturdy enough to sort out any back-posture problems and a radio with a big red button that I was told not to press unless '14 knife-wielding gang members spontaneously attack you, as the entire Met Police force would turn up to save you'. Message received loud and clear. I spent the next few days in constant panic of an accidental button-press.

Looking like I belonged on the set of a gritty police drama, we set off on patrol in Sarah's vehicle with her German Shepherd in the boot. We stopped briefly to meet the rest of her team for breakfast in a greasy spoon café and the morning could not have possibly been more of a fantastic cliché.

Cruising towards Central London, I watched as other cars obeyed the traffic laws slightly better than normal and how everyone always courteously gave way to us. Then the radio broke the peace and barked at us to attend a call – Sarah clicked the sirens on and we were away, 50, 60, 70 mph down London streets with vehicles parting out the way just in time for us to fly through. With my heart pounding and having gone all of 500m, the radio came through again, we weren't needed after all. Admittedly, I was a little disappointed – I was really looking forward to seeing Sarah and her dog in action.

We headed back out of Central London to meet the rest of the team for some afternoon training with the dogs in a school deserted for the holidays. Each officer and their dog took it in turns to enter a school building and search for a second officer who was silently hiding somewhere inside. Within five minutes each dog successfully sniffed out the hidden person. After three of the pairs had gone, the officer in charge of training turned to me and asked if I would like to take a turn hiding. 'Yes' is the only real answer to that question.

Whilst I love dogs and was a big fan of the German Shepherds, I wasn't so keen on the idea of an angry one thinking I was a criminal and coming to sniff me out. Swallowing my nerves, I gave the correct reply and not only said 'yes' but also lied and followed up with 'that sounds amazing, I've always wanted to try that', before I even had the chance to consider what I was saying. Who has ever dreamt of being chased by a police dog? No one. Ever.

Dutifully, though, I put on a jute bite sleeve 'just in case' that weighed nearly as much as me, grabbed a squeaky toy to throw once I had been found (an ironic 'reward' for a snarling, barking beast) and hid in a cupboard on the ground floor.

It was pitch black and silent, the longest three minutes of my life. My arm was sweating and shaking ever so slightly. Can dogs

smell fear? Finally, I could faintly hear the
dog entering the classroom and start sniffing
around. She knew I was there and within a
few seconds had started howling and snarling
right outside the cupboard door to indicate
a person found. As instructed I opened the
door slightly to throw out the squeaky toy and could see nothing
but gnashing teeth and angry dog spittle. In a panic, I refused to
open the door any further and dropped the toy limply on the floor
just outside. Once she had got hold of the reward, she turned back
into a formidable but entirely docile and controllable dog. I came
out with the largest fake smile I could muster and lived another
day.

Once training for the morning was complete, Sarah and I
headed back up into Central London on patrol, and as it was a
quiet afternoon, she took me to visit the stables of the Met Police's
Mounted Branch in Westminster where I was given a full tour,
shown the horses and was told about their care and role within the
police force. Once we had covered their ceremonial role, we talked
about their use in law enforcement and crowd control. It was then
suggested that to better understand what it must be like to work
during a riot, I try on the mounted officer's riot kit.

Although I was grinning at the time, I was barely able to move
due to the sheer weight and bulk of the protective gear. Knowing
that during breakdowns in public law and order, officers must sit in
this for up to eight or ten hours, sometimes through the night with
no bathroom breaks, my respect for them and their horses could
not have been higher.

After an hour with the mounted branch, we were back on
patrol and edging slowly towards South London. Again, the car

radio crackled on loud, calling us to a potential drug find near Brixton. The siren and lights were clicked on and we sped along, dodging cars, pedestrians and bollards. Westminster to Brixton in less than five minutes! This exact route was once my commute home and took at least 50 minutes on a good day, so you see the sort of speed we are talking about.

We pulled up outside a courtyard with low rise, drab blocks of flats on each side. The firearms unit had already made an arrest but suspected that the individual had hidden drugs in the stairwell beforehand; time for Sarah and her dog to step in and get sniffing.

Sarah and her dog entered a brick stairwell that smelled faintly of urine. I tentatively waited with the other police unit, not wanting to add more scents to the mix. A minute passed with nothing. They went up to the first floor – still nothing. The second and final floor led to another minute of silence – nothing.

No drugs were found that day.

As you can probably tell from the gushing, I really enjoyed this placement. I loved the variety of the role – that every hour, let alone every day, could be totally different. Officers don't know what sorts of situations they could be thrown into at any given moment, and whilst this can, undoubtedly, be a difficult thing, it can also be exhilarating and hugely rewarding. Every new situation has to have a tailored approach, so problem solving was a major part of day-to-day life, along with the individual contributions that officers made. I also really enjoyed the camaraderie that comes with working so closely with others in high-pressure circumstances. Their work makes an obvious difference too, and I found that the more I learnt and observed, the more my respect continued to increase. Whilst policing has its issues, in the dog support unit the pros seemed to far outweigh the cons.

COUNTER-TERRORISM POLICE

Based in Wapping, I spent some time with the Marine unit with the Met Police, and it was just as exciting as it sounds. After about two hours navigating the London Underground and Overground networks, I finally made it to a non-descript Victorian building along the Thames. It took me about ten minutes just to figure out how to get in – I must have either looked very suspicious or incredibly naïve, entering my first police station.

Within the marine department, I was going to be spending time with the counter-terrorism team. The squad, almost all of whom were the size and build of rugby players, warmly welcomed me and I felt like I had jumped straight into a police drama TV series. There was an awful lot of team banter, plans for operations covering the walls, and about six separate offers for a very milky cuppa.

A constable showed me around the station, taking me down to the docks to see the numerous high-speed boats that were bobbing around and reeling off marine policing trivia – this was England's first recognised preventative police unit, don't you know? I then hopped in the back of a police van (I won't pretend that I didn't find it incredibly exciting) and headed up with two constables to a central command centre to sit in on their briefing to a larger, land-based counter-terrorism unit that would be joining the team I was with for the day.

En route, I started to ask what it's like to work in counter-terrorism – in recent months, the UK had endured several horrendous major terror attacks in London and Manchester. There is, of course, a huge amount of training, intelligence gathering and analysis that goes on behind the scenes. Part of this is for officers to learn to 'people-watch' effectively – how to pinpoint individuals who are acting suspiciously in crowded public locations. However, I also learned that this doesn't always lead to catching terrorists. It turns out that terrorists and people who feel guilty while nervously waiting for the person they are having an illicit affair with act in a surprisingly similar way.

The operation for the day had two goals – partly to engage the public to reassure and educate on counter-terror issues, and partly to deter any individuals looking to cause harm by placing a highly visible police presence on and around the river.

The units were split in half. One group was tasked with talking to the public along Southbank and the others were given the far less arduous job of being whizzed from the London Eye to the Millennium Dome and back at full tilt.

Wanting to have the opportunity to speak openly with the officers about their careers and life in the police, I was with the half of the unit based on the boat, so spent most of the afternoon on a high-speed cruise. The team's views on life as a police officer were refreshingly candid and decidedly mixed. Many felt that whilst there was the potential for a fulfilling career where you have the opportunity to make a continuing positive impact on communities, it was frequently held back by the constant cuts to the police force. The stress and strain that politics had placed on policing was often making the job one long, demoralising slog. This was exactly what I was hoping not to hear but was what I had expected. Issues such as the massive rise in gun and knife crime (up 42% and 24% respectively in a single year), acid attacks, gang violence and policies on the limited legal protection of police officers chasing vehicles came up again and again. The officers I spoke to seemed desperate to do more to protect the public, but felt that in the current circumstances, it was not always easy to do so.

As we neared the dock, they gave the positives too by reiterating just how rewarding being a police officer can be. The amount of time you spend working in close quarters and in stressful situations with your unit means that they become your family away from home, and the bond between them was obvious by the cheery chitchat. Making London a safer place and protecting the most vulnerable in society is an intensely fulfilling way to spend your working life and the officers were rightly proud of that. Ultimately, it was more about taking a longer-term view of having a positive impact, rather than getting pulled down by cuts, red tape and the political frustrations of the day.

One thing that strongly came across was that no two days are the same – the level of variety working in the police meant that there seemed to never be a dull day in the office. This is one of the benefits of having a more active and less desk-bound job. Several of the officers I spoke to had intentionally decided to remain as constables rather than aim for promotion as they loved the practical side of policing the streets and didn't want to focus on the managerial aspects that seniority brings. Whilst they certainly would have had the experience and ability to work in higher-ranking roles, I had a huge amount of respect for their desire to stay on the beat, making an impact in the way that they felt they could best.

There were a lot of ways in which a career as a police officer would be perfect for me; it certainly would combine being on my feet with making a difference and dealing with strategic issues. The lack of creativity though would frustrate me, as would the strictly hierarchical nature of the institution.

EXPLORER

I decided I would have to take part in a couple of my own adventures – one mini, and one decidedly less mini.

The mini one

I started small, by seeing if someone already doing something adventurous would have me. Luckily, one close to home said yes – Dan Raven-Ellison is a National Geographic Emerging Explorer and describes himself as a 'Guerrilla Geographer'. A few months ago, I joined him for a section of his 563km walk spiralling around London as part of his campaign to make our capital an official National Park City, given that 47% of it is green space.

Whilst this wasn't quite walking to the South Pole, the kilometres I walked with him showed that adventure can be accessible to the masses and is a positive force for good. Dan's project was ultimately advocating for London's green spaces to be conserved, with their natural beauty, wildlife and cultural heritage enhanced for the economic and social benefit of local communities – an aim that I could not support more strongly.

The less mini one

After the excitement of taking part in a mini-adventure, I decided to aim for something a little bigger; I signed up to climb four of Morocco's highest mountains in 48 hours. Mount Toubkal is the highest peak in North Africa, at 4167 metres, and the other three are only marginally smaller. To give you a sense of scale, the UK's tallest mountain is 1345 metres – roughly 30% of the size of Toubkal. Because I never make anything easy for myself, I chose to wait a few months and head to the Atlas Mountains in winter, when temperatures regularly got down to -20°C and a foot of snow wouldn't be unusual. This meant that this particular adventure would be after the end of my yearlong project, but I couldn't resist the challenge (the reason I gave at the time) and really needed another few months to make sure I was fit enough (the real reason).

Training began in earnest.

Living in London, I did not have easy access to many large hills to walk up, so chose to put the treadmill on maximum incline for 30-45 minutes at as high of a speed as I could tolerate at walking speed. I then added some weights to a pack – starting small at 4kg and working my way up to 10kg – and watched endless episodes of Have I Got News For You to try and distract myself from the fact that my legs were on fire. Whenever I had a spare chance at the weekend, I headed up to the Chiltern Hills for some fresh air practice. Add in a couple of sessions of weights and core each week, I was left praying that I was fit enough to not hold the group back.

Fast forward from mid-summer to November 2017, and with many hours spent in Cotswolds Outdoor shop, I landed in Marrakesh airport without the faintest clue of what to expect, though Marrakesh's +28°C was the first pleasant surprise! A somewhat less pleasant one was when most of the group I was about to hike with casually dropped in that they were marathon runners…

Leaving Marrakesh's dusty plain behind, I drove up into the Atlas Mountains to the last outpost town, Imlil. By mid-afternoon, I had stocked up with supplies (mostly Twix-related) and having been up since four in the morning, started hiking up a well-trodden path to the first stop for the night. This first short afternoon hike left me cautiously optimistic – this wasn't too hard, I was still warm enough to be wearing a T-shirt when in the sunshine.

Day 2 stepped up a gear with a full day of hiking up to base camp at 3200 metres. Again, for context, this is the height of the highest ski lift in the highest ski resort in France, so definitely not low in altitude… It got steeper, though not yet intolerably so, and as I began burning plenty of energy, on went some layers and down went the pace; the higher you get, the colder and thinner the air. After a few hours of continuous hours of ascent, it gently started to snow and the vegetation petered out until there was only white-dusted rock. By the end of the eight-hour hike, I was pretty beat, but still left feeling like I would have plenty of energy the next day, after a hot meal and a good night's sleep.

Adventure lesson one: Altitude

The first symptoms of altitude sickness are insomnia and loss of appetite. However, to keep check of your symptoms and health, you must be aware of what is normal and what is abnormal in the first place. This would have been the first lesson – if I'd have been aware of it.

The next morning rolled around brightly and I shook off a surprisingly restless night, given the amount of exercise the day before. After picking at breakfast, we set off for the first day of double peaks – Ras Ouanoukrim (4083m) and Timzguida (4089m). It was a day of over 1000m of ascent, including a few ups and downs, and the temperature steadily dropped – I had never worked so hard physically and been in so many layers of clothes before. The incline of the ascent had increased again by several degrees and I had switched into mountaineering boots for extra foot and ankle support. The hiking poles were out too, mercifully taking up to 25% of the pressure off my knees and giving me a bit of extra balance.

At the top of a major col – the lowest point on a mountain ridge between two peaks – at about two thirds of the way up, I took the first big break for peppermint tea and snacks (it was Morocco after all). I was rewarded with the first half-impression of what the view at the top was going to be like. We were making OK time, the weather was clear, and it already felt like I was on top of the world, looking out over the start of the Sahara below.

There were two sections remaining to reach the first peak; a tricky scramble and a final steep plod to the summit of Ras. I had done some scrambling before in the UK and have found it exhilarating; it is essentially rock climbing that's not quite vertical enough to justify ropes and full climbing gear – at the easy end, at least – but looks like it should unquestionably have both of those things to the untrained eye. Sure-footedness is key. Looking up at the jagged rock formations, in typical gung-ho style (sorry mum), I got going without thinking twice about the sheer drop of several hundred feet on either side.

Adventure lesson two: Trust

To be confident and sure-footed, it turns out you have to have total faith in your kit. New boots with a very unfamiliar tread and untested rigidity, it seems, do not provide that trust. You do not want to be testing these things for the first time at 3800 metres up. This became obvious about five minutes into scrambling up an hour-long section.

My pace dropped as quickly as my confidence.

I fell further and further back among the group, until I was nearly last. I started taking fewer and fewer calculated risks, checking and double checking that every foothold and handhold was secure. Whilst this sounds like thoroughly sensible behaviour, it is only up to a point; when you are up against remaining sunlight hours, falling temperatures, ever-changing weather and ten other people waiting for you, confident decisiveness is critical.

I spent what felt like hours slowly picking my way up to endless ledges and crevices, always being pulled slightly backwards by an over-filled pack. Next time, gloves with finger grips would also be a very useful thing!

Thankfully, there were no mistakes made and I safely made it to the final section, albeit behind schedule. We crossed into 4000m+ territory.

Adventure lesson three: Learn from lesson one

I was left worn out after the excitement of scrambling and found myself becoming less and less able to keep up. Gradually, the gap between myself and the group grew. I also started to develop a headache and then felt nauseous.

Clue: headaches and nausea are also symptoms of altitude sickness.

I am not ashamed to say that it took a monumental effort to walk those last few hundred metres to the summit of Ras, it really did take all my determination to ignore the screaming in my legs and continuing to put one foot in front of the other.

But then, I was at the top. And it really was spectacular. Squinting on the summit of Ras with the most forced smile I had ever mustered.

The decision was made to not attempt the second peak – it turns out I wasn't the only one in the group who had been struggling with an unexpected set of symptoms and the weather was beginning to turn. It would mean that I wouldn't achieve the goal of four in 48 hours, but it was time to be sensible and realistic, for once.

By the time I got back to base camp, several hours later, I really was exhausted. My appetite had entirely disappeared, and I had begun to feel very nauseous. Throwing up later that night, I realised this was bad enough that it would certainly hold the group back and could impact my chance at summiting Toubkal the next day. Fortunately, the guide I was with gave me some Diamox, a medication which reduces altitude sickness symptoms.

What a difference that one tiny pill made.

I started out gingerly the next morning, though felt leagues better than the night before. Over the course of what should have been the most challenging day – climbing over bungalow-sized frozen boulders deep in the shadow of Toubkal – I felt only stronger.

The group had initially been split into two, with the first half striding ahead to summit their third peak, and the half I was in, who took things at a little more of a measured pace and did not aim for the third.

This time, when I passed the 4000m mark and knowing I still had 167 vertical meters of ascent to go, I was totally in control of my body. I had (medically) acclimatised, lightened my pack substantially and gotten better at walking at the much slower pace necessary when the air is thin. I was taking food and water in far more regularly and had finally begun to work out how to wear my layers without constantly stopping to take one off or put one on.

After six hours of going only up, the ground flattened out and, finally, gave up altogether. Blinking half-frozen sweat from my eyes and looking up, I was 4167 meters above sea level and there was nowhere else to go.

The feeling of being at the top of a mountain that you have worked hard to climb is unlike anything else I have experienced.

It's all-consuming, addictive and is a place of clear-headed epiphanies. Ordinarily clichéd statements will take on new meaning, becoming sincere and profound – you can say things like, 'I will write a book', 'I am truly over my ex' or even 'I can push myself further than this' – and really mean them when you get back down again. The summit is a place where you feel as if you can breathe for the first time, even with 40% less oxygen.

In short – I think I found my thing.

This is what I want to do over and over and over again. It won't be possible in the short term, even the medium term, and maybe it will never be possible in the full-time career sense and will have to be as part of a portfolio or purely hobby-based. But, I want to find a way to do all the things that my adventure heroes do too.

BLOGGER

Hear me out, this really is a job.

After I spent 18 months running 25before25, being a blogger was one of the most time-consuming parts of the whole project. From designing, creating and maintaining the site, to writing content and building an audience through social media and the press, it took up a big proportion of time and taught me a whole range of new skills. It also exposed me to the blogging community and to those who do this as their professional career.

It was never part of the original plan to include blogger as one of the 25 careers, but as the year progressed, I realised that whenever anyone asked what I did for a living, I would explain that I was a blogger. It then seemed strange that I would never actually discuss what has become a distinct part of my career and the platform that opened so many doors.

Step one: Learn to design and build a website

This is something I knew absolutely nothing about in any capacity prior to deciding that I wanted to do it, except for copy and pasting html code into MySpace, aged 13. Please do not look that up.

I tried a few platforms like WordPress and SquareSpace, and even though they had beautifully designed templates, they didn't give a large enough degree of autonomy to create what I wanted without paying for a web designer, which was certainly something that did not feature in my non-existent budget.

Several weeks and three or four terrible designs in, I discovered Wix and finally managed to create the first version of the current site. The hosting, domain name and lower tier level accounts came in at about £60 per year, which didn't break the bank. Whilst, of course, the website would look substantially better if I had handed it over to a professional, figuring it out myself was all part of the learning experience and kept costs down!

It was all the tiny details that took the most time, things like the little icon to the left of each internet tab you have open, or how to create a subscriber form pop-up box that isn't going to annoy your users. Then there are things like logos, colour schemes and images, making sure your pages don't take five entire minutes to load, and ensuring the whole thing works well across different operating systems and on mobile phones.

After I had gotten all of that nailed, there was then the question 'how does anyone find my website?' to answer. I had no idea beforehand that you had to physically list it on Google; I had just assumed that it was an automatic thing. Turns out no.

After you have figured that out, you then need it to be listed high enough under your keywords so that someone is likely to click on it. When was the last time you looked at a website on page seven of Google's listings?

All of this took over three months' work in evenings and on weekends.

Step two: The first post

This was the hardest part of the entire project. I wrote and re-wrote that first blog post approximately 37 times and asked at least nine friends to read through the final draft.

Finally pressing 'publish' and putting it on social media for some one thousand people to see was both terrifying and liberating.

Acceptance from your peers is, oddly, far more nerve-wracking than that of abstract newspaper readers.

It took several more months of writing posts before I had the confidence to stop asking a friend or two for their thoughts on everything.

Step three: Social media and subscribers

Someone in their mid-20s should know how to 'do' social media, it should be almost second nature, in theory. I have found this to be true for running your own, personal social feeds (of which I only had one prior to the blog), but not so much for when it's more 'business' focused. This is because, quite simply, running a blog has been more like running a business than I had ever realised.

Social media needs a dedicated amount of time spent in planning and in content creation. Consideration needs to be given to what time of day you are posting, which hashtags will have the most impact and if there are any other influencers you can collaborate with, for example. Whilst professional Instagrammers may make it look like they just decided to spontaneously upload that perfect photo – I assure you that it was likely planned days, if not weeks in advance in a content schedule with 60 other versions of that one image.

I found it a difficult balance to strike and have often got a little frustrated when my blog's success was only measured through how many Facebook likes it got. Especially due to recent changes in Facebook's algorithms, any content I posted was only visible to a tiny fraction of those who followed my page. This led me to experiment with sponsored posts and promoting the page through advertising on Facebook. Whilst this did give a boost in the number of likes and followers, it sometimes didn't feel right that this was the only realistic

way to grow my following on Facebook. It was all a bit of an uphill battle.

In social trends these days, it's all about Instagram. Twitter comes in second, whilst Facebook is a distant third. This is something I have certainly not cracked quite yet, and still needs quite a bit of work. It is also part of the reason I'm trying to build up my subscribers list, as it's (hopefully) a less fickle way to communicate with people interested in the blog.

Step four: Increasing reach

One of the best ways I've found to get ideas out there and grow my blog is through the press, both print and online.

For the most part, this means writing a 'pitch' email, with either an outline, or the fully completed article attached. I spend time researching the most relevant editors across a range of publications which I can submit my work to. This is something I go through phases with, and only spend time on when I have time to spend, as it is not usually a quick process. When an article is accepted, for example with Cosmopolitan, it took eight months of work to go from pitch to publication.

After initially being accepted as a contributor, there are now some publications which I can submit articles directly to without writing the accompanying pitch. Huffington Post is the biggest platform for this, though they reserve the right to decline articles.

Then there is collaborating with other bloggers and relevant online businesses like graduate recruitment site Milkround. This I found much easier to do, as it is mutually beneficial to both parties so a much easier sell.

The biggest obstacle

Almost none of the above included writing posts or articles and finding the time to do this whilst juggling everything else has been tricky, despite it being the most enjoyable. It's a bit of a cycle – the more you grow a platform, the more work it takes to maintain it, which leaves less time for creating the content. But when you do, it helps to grow the platform even more.

All of the above could quite easily have been a full-time job in itself, without working in the 25 jobs throughout the year. This means it's something that frustratingly always ends up getting a little de-prioritised in favour of doing the actual work.

Do I want to be a blogger? Blogging in its purest sense, yes, because I loved having the freedom to write what I wanted and to be as innovative and creative with it as I could be. You can shape it into whatever way you want as running a blog has value, so it can include travel and non-desk-based work – I wrote most of this from a swimming pool in Bali, for example.

I find the dependency on social media frustrating, as managing that successfully is a career in itself and can be highly superficial. There is plenty to suggest that blogging is on its way out after 15 years in the sun and is being replaced entirely by the likes of Instagram and YouTube.

All in all, if I want to make blogging work, I need to find a way to make it work with social media, rather than against it, as these days you can't do one without the other.

CHAPTER SIX

ON NOT CHOOSING
ONE JOB

a jack-of-all-trades is a master of none, but oftentimes better than a master of one.
– old english proverb

The day before my 25th birthday, I completed all 25 placements. It had, without question, been the best year of my life.

I met hundreds, if not thousands of new people, each an inspirational teacher in their own way, with many having dedicated their lives to helping others. The whole experience was incredibly humbling. I got to try so many things that I had previously only been able to dream of, things that I would have once considered totally unachievable to the point of being slightly ridiculous, like archaeology, travel writing and, now, being a published author. It turns out I loved more of them than I had counted on. I guess it was short sighted to think that I could try all of my dream jobs and end up only wanting to pursue one of them.

Spending a year working in so many different types of jobs has fundamentally changed me. I had not grown up as the most confident person, and the idea of letting other people read something I had written, or even worse, hear me speak in public was nightmarish.

I do these things all the time and not only do they no longer terrify me, but I actively enjoy doing them. Stick me in a room with 250 people I don't know and all of a sudden, it's not an intimidating environment but a chance to share my story and inspire others to make a change too. Opening up about myself publicly felt, at first, like I was knowingly exposing myself to ridicule and criticism. Yet, time and time again, it had been validated, first by those I knew and later by many more I didn't.

Mostly importantly, it had been the happiest year of my life. Every day was a joy; every morning I got up and looked forward to the weeks and months ahead. I learnt something new every day and met new people every week. That variety has been so refreshing that it had almost become addictive, it would be difficult to give up.

Fundamentally, I was a different person to who I was the year before. My experiences shaped and changed my views into totally new ones. I found that I could not fit back into the skin of the person I had been not very long ago; I had stretched into an entirely new shape that couldn't be satisfied with my past life. This is hardly a unique experience, it is not the career path that I had once considered that changed, it was me. Plenty of the jobs that I tried over the past year had once been my dreams, but the more I explored, the more my dreams morphed into something new entirely. Knowing now that I must 'make the goal conform to the individual, rather than make the individual conform to the goal', as Hunter S. Thompson wrote in a letter to his friend Hume Logan (you can find the full letter in Appendix 4), I finally feel truly comfortable in who I am.

Plenty of us talk about the old *gap yah* mantra of wanting to 'find ourselves', usually through travelling down the gringo trails of South America or South East Asia. However, the journey I have been on right here at home has taught me how I make sense within my own context. What I have learnt here has far more direct relevance to the rest of my life. I still may not fit into the norm in a traditional sense (and I will absolutely continue to grab any opportunity to see more of the world), but by figuring out who I am as an individual in relation to the world of work, I have realised my own goals rather than trying to shape myself to pre-determined ones.

Opportunity in indecision

The problem I faced on finishing all 25 was that there wasn't just a singular favourite; there had been eight. I loved them for different and often overlapping reasons, but it can be reduced to four core attributes:

1. Creativity, especially writing
2. Innovation
3. Being outdoors and travel
4. Making a difference

It turns out that these four things are the most important career attributes to me, even if two of them started as being secondary.

Hanging over all of these though is variety. I learnt that I intrinsically need to be doing different things as often as is practical, I enjoy being busy and juggling lots of different balls. I love having to totally switch mindset at a moment's notice and having the chance to learn something new each and every day.

EIGHT OF TWENTY-FIVE
The placements I loved most and why

CREATIVITY	INNOVATION	OUTDOORS AND TRAVEL	MAKING A DIFFERENCE
Journalism	Property development	Farming	Crisis management
Author	Farming	Explorer	Police
Travel Writing		Police	Explorer
		Travel Writing	Journalism
		Author	

At this stage of life, I don't want to be comfortable and I don't want things to be too easy. I want to test myself and continue exploring my options, now is the time for my career to be front and centre.

They say that variety is the spice of life. It makes time slow down, monotony is what makes you blink and realise six months has flown by without you noticing. The variety I have experienced over the past year has helped me embrace and appreciate life – I have no intention of giving that up. I want a life of adventures, professionally and literally, or at least that's what I want right now. Variety brings flexibility, so I will reassess in a few years' time and see if my priorities have changed. For now, though, variety is a lifestyle choice and will influence everything about my working life.

Other careers I have tried would also have fit under these headings, but these are the placements I also enjoyed most of all because of the type of work I would be able to do through them, the lifestyle I would be able to lead, or the people I would be able to work with.

After spending weeks mulling over how I could possibly find one job that incorporated all of this, I decided that I wasn't going to choose just one, and that I don't have to. I want a portfolio career – a career made up of multiple jobs in parallel through part-time, freelance and/or contract work. These could be jobs in the same industry or in totally different ones. The type of work could be linked or completely unrelated.

Growing up and going through the education system taught us that we had to choose one job, one skillset, in which we had to specialise. It starts before we even reach our first day of school, when our parents peer down and ask us what we want to be when we grow up – they are expecting only one answer, yet age three, plenty of us automatically list about five different things. When we get to an age at school where we are introduced to careers education, the expectation is the same. Pick one and only one. The concept of picking two or three, or even four, careers simply did not, and still does not, exist.

Let's change this assumption, because you do **not** need to choose just one. You can mix several of your passions with several of your skills. What was labelled as indecision and fickleness as a teenager and young adult can be turned into a strength and into opportunity.

This chapter is about how to design a career that is right for you. This is not about falling into that stereotype of a disloyal millennial with no sticking power, but about how to make the most of your multiple talents, how it will make you a stronger person and a stronger employee overall. This is how to find positive opportunity in what has always been seen as a negative.

That could mean having one job as your 'anchor' of income and stability that is supported by numerous side gigs. Or it could mean using a specific skillset as the anchor that can be applied to several totally unrelated jobs within one industry or in several different industries.[64] It could also be another totally separate combination that works for you. It's about variety, and it is about being the one in control. I wanted full autonomy over my career in as many different ways as possible. This is how I managed it and how you can too.

What came next

At the time of writing, nine months following my 25 jobs, I have worked in six jobs as part of my portfolio career:

1. An author, by writing this book.
2. A public speaker, by regularly speaking to schools, universities and businesses.
3. As a freelance travel writer, specialising in remote travel and mountaineering.
4. As the careers section editor of a national student magazine.
5. In communications for an international development organisation.
6. In social media marketing for an Italian restaurant chain (a little random, but hey, I got to write about Italy and Italian food all day long).

Those are not short-term bits of work experience, but proper paid jobs that I earn an income from. In those, there is an awful lot of writing, much of which I do outdoors, plenty of travel, a fair bit of making a difference and lots of ideas generation, though I'm still working on the entrepreneurialism. I realised my perfect job didn't exist, so I stitched together all the things I wanted to do and crafted my own career path. I don't have one single job title and explaining what I do for a living usually entails a 20-minute conversation.

No two days are the same and whilst some of the jobs have managers, ultimately, I am my own boss. The autonomy is enthralling; being able to carve out my own niche and set my own agenda has been the perfect follow on from exploring so many different careers. It has enabled me to achieve a lifelong goal – publishing my first book, something that would have undoubtedly remained a pipe dream if I had stayed on my original path. Whenever I feel that work is running away from me, I have the flexibility to readdress the balance of my portfolio. I can reduce the amount of time I spend on one project and increase time on another or start an entirely new one to give myself more time outdoors or something that is more geared towards making a difference, for example. I am often also paid contractor and consultancy level fees, as opposed to a salary, which increases my daily rate compared to what it would be as a permanent member of staff.

In terms of my skillset, I am able to develop my strengths and build complementary skills, which can be applied across industries. This makes me a more resilient and flexible worker, who can apply best practices that I have picked up along the way to different situations. Time management and general organisational skills need to be a major strength, as does the ability to build relationships and develop rapport quickly. All of this comes back down to feeling empowered and in control of my own career, and to feel trusted to get on with a job.

Much of this comes back to feeling able to fully express myself. I could never have found a traditional full-time job that would have allowed me to combine my passions for careers education and advice, adventurous travel, climbing mountains and expeditions, with the life-long goal of writing a book. All this whilst also exploring and developing other forms of writing and communications. It has put me on a path to achieving the lifestyle I want and the satisfaction I get from the variety of day-to-day life means I am hugely motivated and productive. For the most part, I am in control of my work/life balance, and I have been known to occasionally take my Saturday and Sunday on weekdays just because I can.

I am not solely dependent on a single job (my former workplace made a third of staff redundant in the months leading up to my resignation) so have found myself feeling more in control of my job security as I have spread my risk between multiple jobs where I know the start and end date. If I were to ever lose one of my portfolio roles, I have plenty to fall back on as I already have multiple other income streams and have honed my employability skills. This also means I'm able to re-invent myself more easily if I start seeing the decline of an industry and the blossoming of another, or as my interests or priorities change over time.

The majority of jobs I do remotely, meaning I can work wherever and within reason whenever I like, as long as the job gets done. That means no offices and no commuting, unless I want to. I had always assumed that I would have to wait until I could find a job in a career that would send me abroad for work to get my travel fix whilst earning a living. Now I realise that I could take matters into my own hands.

Why portfolio careers are good for society

Portfolio careers are undergoing an image change. Loyalty to one company is increasingly being thrown out of the window, along with the view that those choosing to jump ship are betraying that company. Already over 60% of us have had the same number of jobs by our late 20s as the majority of our parents will have had in their lifetime.[65] Crucially, there is a predicted shift towards positively viewing employees with multiple skillsets, who can easily move across functional boundaries.[66] This does not necessarily equate to a workforce of generalists (not that being a generalist is a bad thing by any means) but could instead mean a workforce made up of specialists able to apply their core skills across multiple sectors. In other words, an army of people with portfolio careers.

This is supported by research elsewhere. 94% of millennials in one global survey said they were open to a portfolio career. Alternative career structures like this are so highly prized by young people because we value learning new skills, the higher salary that having a portfolio career or going freelance brings and the control we get over both our careers and our work/life balance. Older millennials (25-34) are also very much driven by a desire for meaning and purpose in their work too. This is true for younger millennials too (18-24), but in a slightly less statistically significant way. Given that 65% of the jobs that younger millennials will have don't even exist yet, that desire for the continued learning of new skills is also absolutely critical for a country's workforce and economy, as well as for the employability and security of young people's careers. A thirst for learning new skills even after formal education will keep us all ahead of the curve, the future of work depends on that. The graph below illustrates reasons why people choose portfolio careers.[67]

As portfolio career aficionado and journalist Christina Wallace put it: 'The world is changing faster than ever before, and entire industries are at risk as AI, machine learning, autonomous vehicles, and other technologies go from the fringe to mainstream. Specialising in just one industry could be limiting at best and catastrophic at worst. Diversification across skills and industries is the only way to stay nimble and relevant.'[68]

The graph below illustrates the different reasons why people choose portfolio careers.

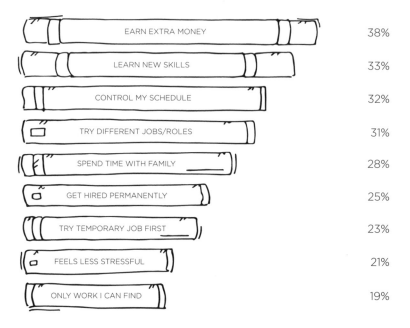

EARN EXTRA MONEY	38%
LEARN NEW SKILLS	33%
CONTROL MY SCHEDULE	32%
TRY DIFFERENT JOBS/ROLES	31%
SPEND TIME WITH FAMILY	28%
GET HIRED PERMANENTLY	25%
TRY TEMPORARY JOB FIRST	23%
FEELS LESS STRESSFUL	21%
ONLY WORK I CAN FIND	19%

Add to this the aging population demographic of most developed countries, it means that our work lives are going to become an ultra-marathon that requires us to continuously be able to re-invent ourselves. Within the next five years, it is predicted that the workforce will have significantly higher levels of individuals with 'skill sets in multiple simultaneous careers (79%) and more than half of all workers being temporary, on contract or freelance (60%).'[69] This needs to be embraced.

Considering this at a more strategic level, a nationally mobile workforce that can move between sectors, either sequentially or in parallel as part of a portfolio career (with the associated benefits from enjoying their jobs), is a workforce that would be incredibly effective. It is a workforce with no single point of failure and one which is more able to withstand the economic and political shocks and changes we are experiencing with increasing frequency. It is a workforce that will be able to avoid that risks that come with groupthink because it will have the breadth of experience to spot and challenge otherwise unseen assumptions and corporate cultural norms. It is a workforce that will be more able to fully embrace innovation and collaboration due to its increased versatility.

Diversifying our working lives is likely to make us happier too. Instead of causing conflict, having multiple passions has been proven to have a 'significant' positive impact on wellbeing, according to a fantastically titled study called 'Can Passion be Polyamorous?' in the Journal of Happiness Studies (which is an actual thing).[70] As we have already established, this is not because people earn more, though, of course, that is always an added bonus. Rather, much of it comes down to the feeling of being able to fully express yourself in a professional capacity, every part of you, whilst offering you control over your work/life balance. Translated into practicalities, this means people with portfolio careers take far fewer sick days and have a notably higher morale. From an employer's perspective, it also means empowering highly mobile staff members that are able to work across time zones without the expense and logistics of multiple offices.[71]

A change in mentality is needed during careers education; young people don't necessarily need to solely aim to be a 'high achiever', but can also or instead aim to be a 'wide achiever'.[72] The idea of being a Renaissance soul or a polymath was once one of the greatest compliments – someone who was able to draw on a vast knowledge base from different subject areas to solve complex problems. We do not sneer at Leonardo Da Vinci and Galileo for their versatility, we celebrate them, and so too should we be encouraging this trait in our young people and ourselves.

The concept of portfolio careers also provides a solution to the issue that many of us experience in our working lives; the gaping expanse between our expectations and the reality of the job we are in. The larger the unmet expectation, the less satisfied and fulfilled we are likely to be; you will not find happiness in a job that you find to be meaningless, no matter how hard you are looking.[73] We need to begin by challenging the expectations we have of our careers – I have said it before and I will say it again: there is no such thing as a Prince Charming job.[74] Your baseline assumption should not be to expect fairy tales and fireworks in your job.

No job is perfect; everyone has bad days and has to make compromises. If your expectations are that high, changing jobs is unlikely to make you happier; it is doubtful that one job will be able to provide you with all that you need to feel happy and fulfilled professionally.[75] What job will pay you a good salary with regular increases; meaning, purpose and work that you are genuinely passionate about; opportunities for continued growth, learning and promotion; flexibility in how you work; valuing and trusting in all of your opinions and ideas; great colleagues that will become lasting friends, and plenty more besides? If you have this job and are still reading this book, then there must still be something about it that niggles away in the back of your mind. Instead of expecting all this and more, split it up into its constituent parts – into smaller pieces.

Consider if you had three concurrent jobs. From one you get the good salary, promotion and trust in your ideas. Another might give you great colleagues, flexibility and continued learning. The third is where you find your meaning and purpose; it also makes you feel valued. Each of these three jobs on their own has their downsides; one might not have colleagues that you can have some banter with, one gives you no personal development and the third is never going to give you a raise or a bonus. But, by spreading your expectations across different jobs, you are able to tick all – or nearly all – of your boxes, everything that is important to you. Those things that would be major drawbacks if you were in one of those jobs permanently, just don't seem to matter as much when you only do it for a day or two a week.

It is best, though, not to apply this particular point to our dating analogy from previous chapters – cheat on your boss, not your partner.

The expectations that our employers have of us need to change too. We need to move away from employment contracts that make it difficult to have a side-gig, or ban them all together, as well as jobs that will require us to sign over ownership of our intellectual property.[76] Adaptability, continued learning and innovative problem solving are what will get millennials and generation z through the seismic changes coming at us for the duration of our working lives; businesses and governments need to embrace alternative ways of working that most encourage these skills and attributes if we want to keep ahead. We need a tax system and workers' rights that enable professional versatility and self-employment to flourish, rather than stifling it.

It is much harder for a self-employed person to get a mortgage, for example, as well as complexities around tax, national insurance and pensions. The rise of the gig economy is slowly leading to changes in legislation.[77][78] There is even a hashtag for it now which is, of course, the 21st century way of knowing something is actually an important issue, #GigResponsibly. Despite the prominence of the gig economy in the media, only 20% of people who would benefit from reformed self-employment rights fit into the archetypal category of delivery drivers with companies like Uber; 60% are professionals like lawyers, consultants and IT specialists who need appropriate worker rights and protection too.[79] With 15% of UK workers now self-employed – that's 4.8 million – we are now starting to see the promise of major changes in rights, but much more will need to be done in the coming decade for the UK economy to be able to fully embrace new and alternative ways of working for a more future-facing workforce.[80][81]

Businesses that have become used to expecting a lifetime of service with little emphasis on employee fulfilment in return will struggle to recruit and retain their young staff – even in spite of 'good' training perks.[82] A much higher degree of collaboration between business leaders and policy makers is needed though to find the right balance of responsibility and flexibility for all of us. There needs to be a reassessment of traditional worker benefits, which need to be moulded around the 21st rather than 20th century. A more enabling and responsive approach rather than a preventative one is needed.[83]

Alternative ways of working like portfolio careers provide the chance to turn millennial dissatisfaction and disloyalty into an opportunity – an opportunity to create a more resilient workforce.[84] This book started by showing how the social contract between employers and the younger generation is broken, and it is ending by showing how workforce resilience through portfolio careers and alternate ways of working can replace that covenant with one that is in everyone's best interest.

Living the dream?

It was a cold and wet January in London. There hadn't been a single dry, sunny day in over a month. I had finished my 25 jobs nearly five months ago and mid-winter blues were kicking in hard, making my feet itchy to go somewhere else, preferably somewhere above 20°C. Usually this is the point where I would start looking at summer holidays and imagining myself in a far less grey part of the world. This year, however, I knew I wouldn't have much time for holidays as I was kick-starting my portfolio career.

To solve the problem, I started Googling to see what my options could be. I got deep into a Google hole. The result was discovering the idea of being a digital nomad. I had heard the term before, so knew that it was someone who works remotely online, so can work anywhere in the world, but I had not considered it as something that I might seriously be able to do. But right now, it seemed like a marvellous idea, and one that I couldn't get out of my head. Maybe I could escape to a tropical paradise and work there too?

Tentatively, I started looking at co-working spaces, the temporary homes of many transient digital nomads. One place kept coming up again and again while I was searching: Bali. I had never really thought about Bali as a travel destination, all I had ever heard about it was the stereotype of an Australian Ibiza and that didn't exactly appeal to me. Further research changed my mind though. It turns out that Bali is also one of the fastest growing start-up hubs in Asia and therefore a haven for digital nomads.[85] That was something that made me sit up and take notice.

Could I really leave miserable London behind and replace it with Bali for a few beautiful weeks? I tested the waters with my jobs and asked if I could hypothetically, theoretically, maybe, please, work on the other side of the planet for a month? To my amazement, they all came back with a resounding yes. I managed to find a co-working space that had faster and more reliable Wi-Fi than I had at home. I also reasoned that because of the eight-hour time difference, if I was given work to do late one afternoon UK time, I would have it done by the time my boss woke up the next morning. All of this certainly helped to swing the argument.

I planned to head out in early March, which was in between the wet and dry seasons but still had off-peak flight prices. I calculated that my flights, accommodation and food would add up to about the same, if not slightly less per month than living in London, especially once I factored in bills, public transport, food and socialising costs, on top of rent. It suddenly seemed to be a no-brainer.

Without thinking much more about it, I booked my flights and accommodation with the co-working space and a few weeks later landed in Bali. It didn't take long to settle in – it's not hard to adapt to the constantly beautiful 30-degree heat, fresh dragon fruit smoothies in the morning and working in a swimming pool. My winter blues and long nights had instantly been replaced by lunchtime yoga sessions, evening surf lessons and trying to ride a scooter.

In terms of productivity, I was initially nervous that I wouldn't be able to concentrate and instead

would be constantly tempted to be a tourist. However, one of the main benefits of a co-working space is being surrounded by other people who are working as hard as you, rather than backpackers just passing through. That everyone was staying at least a month helped too as I had time to build friendships and get to know the highs and lows of their working lives, as they did mine. On many days I ended up working harder and longer than I would have at home, as my work schedule revolved around getting the job done and was influenced by the other people in the co-working space. If they were working into the evening, then I found myself doing so too. Mentally, I was strict about not thinking of this as a holiday, because it was absolutely not. It was a change of scenery for my working life.

On weekends, I got to do all the sightseeing I wanted, driving across the small island to see temples, waterfalls and rice paddy fields aplenty. I managed a short trip over to the nearby Komodo Islands to see the infamous Komodo Dragons and to swim with a shoal of Manta Rays.

There are downsides to this life, though, if you are doing it for more than a month at a time. You miss major life events at home; attending a friend's wedding means flights that can cost hundreds of pounds, for example, so it can be hard to maintain friendships in the way you would if you lived in the same city. Meeting a partner who is in it for the long-term can be hard too, with everyone moving to opposite ends of the world every few months. Then, there is the slightly more gnarly issue of how and where you pay tax. In the UK, for example, you have to pay tax for a certain number of years to be entitled to a state pension. It's an issue that feels like it belongs in the distant future, but it's something worth considering sooner rather than later.

Putting all the cons aside, digital nomads stand to gain a huge amount by living the lifestyle they do; they earn in £ or $, but if they spend rupees they are able to save a much higher proportion of their salary than if they were living in a major western city. And, of course, they aren't tied to a specific place – it's the ultimate way to see the world while you earn. That month it was Bali, but for my digital nomad friends, next month could be Malaysia, Mexico or Morocco.

My month working in the sun contributed to my changing perspective on what it means to have a career, and what is the 'right' way to work. There are, of course, plenty of professions that this sort of lifestyle just won't work for at the moment, but digital nomads are challenging age-old assumptions by using technology to their advantage. They are proving that you can work anywhere on any schedule, as long as you have a decent internet connection. They don't need to play by traditional rules of work and instead are forging their own path, from swimming pools while sipping coconuts.

This does make it all sound very idyllic, but as with anything, there are downsides too. This is mostly about uncertainty – there is less job security in the traditional sense, and even though contract work pays more, it often excludes benefits like holiday pay. These sorts of job relatively easy to come by, though, and I found three of my roles this year through Facebook groups and LinkedIn.

Different working environments might take getting used to. Whilst working remotely from home, or anywhere you like, might sound perfect, loneliness can be a real issue that can negatively impact on mental health.[86] Consider co-working spaces or working in public places like cafes and libraries to try and prevent this; making friends who have similar working patterns is incredibly motivating. When not working with others, I organise to meet a friend for lunch near their office and spend the day working in that area, arrange regular evening social plans to balance things out. You might decide that, actually, you want one of your jobs to be office-based.

Staying focused can also be a challenge; home life can be very distracting. Working remotely means you need to be self-motivated as there is no one physically there to hold you to account. It can be all too easy to promise yourself that you will just watch one episode of something over lunchtime and then find yourself half a season deep. On the plus side, though, you don't have to explain yourself for taking it a little easier for a couple of days each month for period cramps, for example. I have a rule to try to prevent at least one of these issues: no TV during the working day under any circumstances.

Practically, an alternative career can make finances difficult to plan – I don't know what I'm going to be earning in six months or a year's time, for example. I have a rough estimate as I have a daily rate that I charge for most of my work, and as I gain more experience this will increase proportionately. Most jobs don't cover things like paid holiday, sick leave and pensions – you are only paid for the days you work and you don't have access to the same employment rights like protection from unfair dismissal.[87][88] You also need to deal with increased admin in terms of tax, getting a mortgage and sorting out your own pension.

There is a fail safe in knowing that if I absolutely had to, I now have enough experience and contacts that I could apply for a full-time contract or permanent job that would support me financially. 80% of freelancers have said that this is the case for them too; alternative ways of working are a conscious choice and are by no means a last resort.[89] Contracting jobs can move very quickly; I have gone from applying for a job to starting the role in a week. Learning to embrace uncertainty, even enjoying the adrenaline rush of it, has been paramount.

How to have a portfolio career

What if you quite like a few of the career options you have explored and don't want to choose just one of them? How do you actually go about getting the elusive and mythical portfolio career?

You have infinite different combinations of part-time, contract, freelance or whatever sort of side-gig you can think of, and you can mix them up in any order you like. This can be anything from a full-time job with your Sunday afternoons spent cycling with Deliveroo or creating handmade cards to sell on eBay. Over the course of one year, I have had a full-time fixed term contract, a part-time fixed term contract that kept getting extended every month, and a freelance monthly rolling contract. I also had two months where I was hired to work 24/7, but never signed a contract and several different freelance jobs where work was driven by me alone (author, travel writing, public speaking). Some of these overlapped and some of them didn't; I spent months doing nothing apart from writing the manuscript for this book and I also spent months juggling four jobs at once.

You can decide if you want to be a specialist or a generalist, narrowing down to one skillset and/or industry, or choosing a range of entirely different and contradictory jobs. Ensuring that the working environments you choose are right for you is critical too and you shouldn't lose sight of this in the excitement of new jobs. Your portfolio career is what you make of it and you will find a rhythm and balance that works for you. You can use it as an opportunity to further test the water of careers or skills that you have sampled through work experience. The next stage is thinking about how you can begin creating this for yourself.

You are no longer selling just your CV. The chances are that you need to be marketing yourself almost as a brand. If you want to work in a creative industry, think about building a basic website that showcases some of your work and presents your CV in a slightly more creative way than a piece of A4.

When applying for specific jobs you will have to cherry pick the experiences that are most relevant to that job. Your whole CV should be tailored to it, especially your profile at the header. In this, you need to consider what your unique selling point (USP) is – what's so special about you? For each job you want to take on, you can have a different USP.

Having gaps on your CV can be a worry, with time spent on a career break or not in full-time, permanent work. This is something I am usually asked about in job interviews and generally when speaking about my career so far. The answer I give is that the time out that I have had gave me the space to deeply consider and explore all of my options, which means that am now sure that **this** is exactly what I want to be doing now. I have actually gone and tried all the different jobs that I have wondered about and now I really know that this is the one for me. I then talk about how it marries my skills with my passions, interests and experience.

If you are considering a portfolio career, reflect upon the following question.

What are the different types of jobs or skills you would think about doing, if you are considering doing more than one?

Make a list. This could include skills like writing or coding, or jobs like user experience, photographer, graphic designer, driver, or a management consultant, for example.

Much of the networking advice recommended in Chapter Four can be applied to job-hunting too. Use Twitter and Facebook groups, along with messaging individuals on LinkedIn and joining industry specific discussions and groups, making sure that your messaging is consistent between your Twitter bio, LinkedIn profile and your website, if you have one. You will be building on all of those networking techniques – going to events, handing out business cards, arranging coffees, and so on. Having spent time trying out a range of careers, you will have already started to build up a book of contacts; these are relationships that you can now start utilising for jobs. Whenever you do meet people, ask them who else they can introduce you to. You now have a specific purpose for all of these soft skills, bring them out in targeted force.

Depending on the industry you are interested in, recruitment agencies can help, as there will be some that focus on short-term contracts and part-time work. Research to see if this might be something that you could use to your advantage. I got one role through a recruiter who approached me on LinkedIn whose agency happened to focus on short-term public sector contracts – two weeks after signing with them, a role came up that was part-time in social media for an international development organisation, I was the first person the agency called.

If you are interested in starting your own business, there is a huge amount of free support available to young entrepreneurs, including both advice and funding. The Prince's Trust and UnLtd offer both of these, as do most universities to their alumni for the first few years after graduation. Private companies like Virgin Media and O2 also offer this guidance and start up loans, as do some local councils.

All of this may take time, so be patient as it's unlikely to happen overnight. It took me three months to build up from no jobs to having enough work to be the equivalent of working full-time and with a salary higher than I had been earning before. Things can move very quickly though, so don't panic if you are a few weeks in and haven't gotten very far yet. Having a small pot of savings to tide you over for a couple of months can take the pressure off, which you can build up over time before you jump ship. You could also do this by giving your employer three months' notice, which means you have a salary and three months to get yourself sorted. Could you go down to part-time in your current role, while you build up other types of work, for example? Having a supportive network of friends and/or family is helpful especially at this point, as having some emotional support and people that you can rely on to be your sounding board is invaluable. If you would rather have some objective advice, look for coaching and mentoring opportunities through the contacts you have made or charities that focus on career and employability skills.

At the other end of the spectrum, make sure you don't over commit yourself by saying yes to every exciting opportunity that comes your way. I fell into this trap and spent a couple of months working six and a half days a week. Whilst I really enjoyed what I was doing and the people that I was working with, I quickly realised that I was losing sight of my work/life balance. One of the great things about portfolio careers is their flexibility; I was able to take stock and re-adjust my balance of work by reducing hours in one of the roles and pausing another for a couple of months.

Juggling several different jobs at the same time is all about time management, prioritisation and organisation. These are the three absolutely critical skills needed to master multiple jobs in potentially entirely different careers. Setting aside specific blocks of time to do each job helps; it is far more difficult to manage two or three roles when you can be called upon at any time to do any of them.

If you are the one in charge, you get to decide how you prioritise your time. There needs to be time when you can switch off completely and aren't constantly checking emails or answering calls and are instead focusing solely on friends, family and hobbies. This 'off' time needs to be away from both your jobs and from hunting for new opportunities.

All about the money

Being self-employed does mean that there are a few more pieces of life admin to do than you would have otherwise. It can be a bit of a pain and sounds daunting to begin with, but it's a necessary evil that, in reality, will only take up a small amount of your time after you have gotten everything set up and, overall, it's worth it.

Once you have figured out your plan of action in terms of work and jobs, you will need to consider exactly how you want everyone to pay you. First off, if you are paying tax in the UK, you will want to research whether to set up as a sole trader, a limited company or if you will need an umbrella company. Depending on the complexity of your situation, it will most likely be worth asking the advice of an independent accountant. Most won't charge for a first meeting. Each option comes with a different set of pros, cons and responsibilities and which one you choose will depend on your specific circumstances.

It can be more complicated to get a mortgage approved when you're self-employed. Sole traders, company directors and contractors are each assessed by banks in different ways. Generally, you will need to be able to provide two years' worth of financial statements showing consistent earnings (three years is even better, though some lenders will consider you if you only have one year of accounts), something which is often difficult for freelancers who are more likely to have peaks and troughs in earnings.[90] Focus on building up the best possible credit score you can and having consistent evidence to demonstrate that you can afford mortgage payments. Allow for extra time in getting a mortgage approved.

It may seem an awful long way off when you are focusing on saving for a deposit for your first home, but you will also need to think about putting aside a percentage of your earnings for a pension. You will have to choose your own pension scheme and you probably won't have access to employer contributions, as you would if you were a permanent employee (though part-time permanent employees will have access to this) and having an irregular income pattern can make saving difficult. There are tax breaks though for the self-employed; for every £100 you put into a pension, the government will add £25; the earlier you start, the more you will save.

The best pension option for you will depend on your personal needs and circumstances, so it is worth speaking to a regulated independent financial advisor, such as the Money Advice Service, for detailed advice. Though it feels ridiculous when you can't even save for a house deposit, the earlier you start putting money aside for a pension, the better. With an ageing population, we cannot assume that the state pension will be enough to live on when the time comes.

The financial side of things can sound like a lot to take on, but it's not something you immediately need to sort out when you are just starting out on an alternative career path. It is more to bear in mind for once you start having a regular income and reach the point of needing to complete a tax return. Mortgages and pensions are topics to have in the back of your mind for a little further down the line.[91]

Points for consideration

- Portfolio career: a career made up of multiple jobs in parallel through part-time, freelance and/or contract work.
- Variety brings flexibility; variety is a lifestyle choice.
- The concept of picking multiple careers simply did not exist during education.
- Diversification across skills and industries is the only way to stay nimble and relevant.
- A thirst for learning new skills even after formal education will keep us all ahead of the curve, the future of work depends on that.
- We can be wide achievers instead of high achievers.
- Adaptability, continued learning and innovative problem solving are what will get millennials and generation z through the seismic changes coming at us.
- Cheat on your boss, not your partner.
- Portfolio careers provide the chance to turn millennial dissatisfaction and disloyalty into an opportunity – an opportunity to create a more resilient workforce.
- Digital nomads are showing that you don't need to play by traditional rules of work – instead, they are forging their own paths, from swimming pools while sipping coconuts.
- It is critical to make sure that the working environments you choose are right for you.

Questions to reflect on

- What are the different types of jobs or skills you would like to include in your portfolio career?

- What is your elevator pitch?

- In terms of networking, who can you call on? What events could you attend over the next few months? How can you use social media? Are there any companies you would specifically like to target?

- Could you go down to part-time in your current role, while you build up other types of work, for example?

AUTHOR

Career 25 – I am now an author.

That's a sentence that I never dreamed I would actually write. I have been working on The Radical Sabbatical since June 2017 and have been in talks about it since November 2016. It has finally come to fruition.

It all started on day seven of 25before25, when I ran into an old friend's mother, someone I have known since I was four years old, and she said to me, 'there is a book in this'. I laughed it off as a kind comment. Then a couple of other people said it. Then a few more.

Three months later, the project was featured in The Telegraph. Within hours, I got an email through the contact form on my website from a literary agent in New York encouraging me to write a book about the story and asking if she could represent it. That's one mind-blowing email to receive for anyone, especially someone who has always dreamed of writing a book. There is a family video of my parents asking me, aged seven, what I want to be when I grew up. I said with the total conviction that only young children have, that I wanted to be an author.

Giddy with excitement, I signed with the agent and started to keep a journal of my experiences, thinking through what I might write. Six months later, I got an email saying she was no longer able to represent me as she was leaving the industry altogether and changing career. Ironic, right? This meant that if I wanted the book to happen, I was going to have to write full proposal with sample chapters and then start trying to convince another literary agent to take me on. As I later realised, this is often just as hard, if not harder, than getting a book deal with a publisher.

Literary agencies act as the first filter for publishers and getting over this initial major hurdle was big step. It certainly wouldn't have been one that I would have thought I could attempt if it weren't for having already signed with one.

Incentivised by a competition being run by a London agency with a very close deadline, I wrote the whole 50-page proposal and sample chapters in a week, in a deep state of flow. I then sent it out to over 20 agencies and waited.

Within a couple of weeks, I already had replies trickling back in.

No, thank you.

Not for us.

Good luck, I'm sure someone else will take this.

Rejection.

Rejection.

Rejection.

Rejection after disheartening rejection.

After a month and a half, I had given up hope. Virtually all the agencies had replied and said they weren't interested. I reasoned that the ones who hadn't replied yet hadn't done so because they weren't interested.

A full two months later, and weeks before I finished the 25before25 project, someone said yes.

An email came through from an agent who had been out the office for weeks on a holiday, she asked if the project was still available. Yes, it most certainly was! I cried a little bit from excitement.

We arranged to meet that week in central London.

I put on my best pair of heels and tottered through a spotless glass reception and into a mirrored lift. When it opened, I walked straight into an office built to resemble a library. It felt a bit like coming home. I signed with them on the spot.

Next came the process of editing the proposal and then sending it out to publishers, at the same time as trying to build my portfolio career having now turned 25. All of this took about three months, and again, there were lots of rejections to contend with. It wouldn't be an author's story without it. The proposal had been with publishers for a month, and in the same way as with literary agencies, I realised that if I hadn't heard by then, I probably wasn't going to.

A week before Christmas things were at their bleakest, I was terrified that it just wasn't going to happen, after the idea had been seemingly so within my grasp.

I was at one of my work Christmas parties listening to a carol service, mulled wine in one hand and a mince pie in the other after feeling down all week. The choir started to sing the atmospheric Walking in the Air and half way through, my phone buzzed.

It was an acceptance email from a publisher wanting to make an offer.

I immediately cried and gracefully spilt the mulled wine down my sweater in the rush to read the full email while making as little sound as possible. I am an emotionally driven person, if you hadn't noticed – a wreck at weddings.

Receiving an offer on my book and then, a month later, physically signing the deal are quite possibly the best moments of my life to date.

In the interceding months, I wrote this book alongside the rest of my portfolio career. I learnt a huge amount about the publication process, which is something I knew absolutely nothing about beforehand. When there is talk of publicists, booksellers, literary fairs and cover designs, it still feels a little like a dream.

There is definitely a bit of Imposter Syndrome going on – I occasionally wonder if it's actually happening to someone else, and I'm just along for their ride.

But, you have this book in your hands now, either literally or digitally, so it must be real – and this book is the product of the final career, number 25.

CHAPTER SEVEN

ON CHANGE

Our world is never the same as it was the day before. An uncertain political and economic climate for our entire adult lives, partnered with the relentless pace of technological advancement, has changed the nature of work.

It has necessitated a shift from the 9-to-5 and job-for-life expectations that our parents and grandparents grew up with, to the increasing prerogative of exploration and flexibility. Above all, though, it is about fulfilment.

For us millennials, our baseline assumptions about work have fundamentally shifted, and along with them, our expectations of the workplace. Where baby boomers and generation x were in a position to simply be happy to have a job, knowing that it would provide for all of theirs and their families' needs, we no longer see that as a viable option – because it rarely is a viable option.

Working patterns and promises from generations past are no longer upheld and continuing to pretend that they are is counter-productive on a personal level, but also on a national one.

Just taking a payslip home at the end of each month is not enough to keep us engaged and productive at work and – dare I wish it – happy. Not only that, but it is actively making us miserable. The social contract has been broken.

How can we as individuals, communities, companies, industries, sectors and a nation expect to be competitive when so many of us are unhappy in our daily grind? Therefore, we expect a new trade-off. We expect to have fulfilment on a personal scale.

That means fulfilment can be something different for you as it is for me. For some, it will mean flexible working even if they don't have children, for others it will be positive culture or employers that invest in them through training and perks. For others again, it will mean the option of being a wide-achiever rather than high-achiever, with all of the benefits that a portfolio career brings. Some will want to be specialists, but with access to the opportunity to work remotely from another country every now and again.

There are endless combinations. Virtually all of us, though, also want to ensure that we are future-facing, with a skillset that will still be relevant in 20 years' time.

Work must change, both because the world of work is changing, but so are we as the workers. We must unapologetically embrace our demands and expectations in order to build a workplace that moves beyond the persistent industrial revolution approach to one appropriate for the digital revolution.

AFTERWORD

Today, I turned 26 and it's been a year to the day since I finished my radical sabbatical.

Six weeks ago, I found a job advert that read: 'hours will be irregular, frequent, if not 24/7, and working conditions aboard our yacht may be difficult, verging on tough'. I applied.

Right now, I am sitting on a boat in Dartmouth, Devon, working as a writer for a two-month contract over the summer. I am sailing from Land's End to Dover, following the UN Patron of the Oceans and endurance swimmer, Lewis Pugh, as he swims the length of the English Channel. We are campaigning for cleaner and better protected oceans and have been able to meet the Prime Minister, the Secretary of State for the Environment and Prince Charles in person, successfully lobbying for change.

I am on an adventure that is making a positive difference and I am working outdoors constantly. I'm using the skills that I love by ghost writing a blog that is read by two million people a day. It is hard work that is mentally draining – there are no days off and I regularly work 18-hour days. But I'm valued for my skills and feel that I am personally adding more value than I ever dreamed I could at such an early stage of my career.

It is a job that ticks every box and a job that I could never have imagined existing on this day two years ago, and certainly not when sitting in a career talk as a teenager.

This is just one job that was added to my portfolio in the three months in between writing the last chapter and this Afterword. I love what I do and this is one of many roles where I am applying my passion and skills to a cause I care about.

The rest of the time, I work as a writer and public speaker, advocating for careers education that includes multiple work experience placements in a diverse range of industries. I spend a lot of time campaigning for alternative and more flexible ways of working, especially for portfolio careers.

The hope is that this book will help give others the confidence to make a change where they are unhappy or to seek out a different path by showing that it absolutely can be done.

Happiness and fulfilment were the goals when I set out two years ago today, though they felt unachievable then.

It didn't hit me all at once, but crept up on me, slowly – I am now profoundly happy and feel deeply fulfilled. It was subtle at first, but gradually it became the overriding feeling and has never really left. It makes everyday life that bit better

I still have days that aren't so great (I never found that Prince Charming job – turns out I get seasick, so boat life might not be the long-term answer), but instead of having genuinely awful days, there are just days that aren't quite as good as the best days. Work can still be stressful and frustrating, and I spend far more time doing it than I ever did before.

The difference is that, more often that not, it doesn't feel like work.

I have no regrets about quitting my job and trying something different. When you start walking down a path, you rarely know where it might take you, and that's no bad thing. I have embraced a slightly more edge-of-my-seat lifestyle and I'm a different person for it – ironically, I am a far more relaxed one. Sometimes I think back to the person I was then and the person I am now. Often, I don't recognise her, she has changed so fundamentally.

I can say with total confidence that if I turned the clock back, I would do it all over again, without a moment's hesitation.

Every day I wake up and look forward to the day ahead and I regularly struggle to sleep from the excitement of what my next day brings, with small amounts of adrenaline pulsing through me.

These days, that is my Sunday night feeling.

ACKNOWLEDGEMENTS

It starts well, then I get a bit soppy. Sorry, not sorry.

I want to begin by thanking all the companies that let me work for them for such a short period of time, and then let me write my honest thoughts on what I thought it was like to work for them and post it online. That takes some courage and a real commitment to wanting to help young people:

Exeter University Archaeology Department, Oasis Overland, Gypsy Westwood Photography, Bradt Guides, London Lofts, Moor View Alpacas, The Telegraph, A4ID, British Council, The Guernsey Literary and Potato Peel Pie production team, Beechwood Park School, Joshua Design Group, NLGN, Anthea Harrison Garden Design, Raw TV, the Metropolitan Police, MakeMyHouseHome, Sort, Dan Raven-Ellison, Explorer's Connect and afterwards, CoWorkSurf.

Thank you to those who let me interview them – Josh, George, Debbie and the countless people I spoke to while working in the 25 jobs.

From John Catt, thank you to Alex, Meena and the production team. Thank you too, to Ruth and David. This really was a team effort.

The biggest thank you goes to my agent, Tessa, without whom this book would never have been written. You have been hugely supportive every step of the way, constantly going above and beyond to get the best for both me and the book. I could not ask for a better person to work with, here's to the future.

To the many friends who have been constantly supportive throughout what has been a rollercoaster over the past two and a half years, thank you: Alex, Calum, Charlotte, Hayda, Julia, Katie, Katrina, Kish, Mez, Sabah, Sakina, Sarah and Vicky.

Particular mentions to Emily and Tobi for being brilliant, patient sounding boards for the ideas, structure and eventual content of this book.

There have been plenty of people who have acted as mentors over the past few years, thank you especially to Danny, Lewis and Dave. Your faith in me gave me confidence at times when mine was waning.

H.B. – who encouraged me to carry on writing when I had decided I was useless, aged 15. You will likely never read this, but your kind words meant more than I think you ever realised.

To my parents and sister, Mandy, Simon and Katie – without your love and belief, I wouldn't be anything like the person I am today. You have continuously and unwaveringly supported me in the bizarre and unpredictable journey that is my life, while many others might have been more questioning. I can't say thank you enough.

Lastly, thank you to my Grandma, Pauline. You are the writer of the family and have been encouraging me ever since I wrote my first story as a small child. Because of you, the pipe dream of writing a book always felt like it might just be within grasp. I promise there will be a fiction book one day.

REFERENCES

[1] Barrett, H. (2017) *Plan for five careers in a lifetime*. (The Financial Times) Available at: www.ft.com/content/0151d2fe-868a-11e7-8bb1-5ba57d47eff7

[2] Right Management. (2015) *The Flux Report*. Available at: www. rightmanagement.co.uk/wps/wcm/connect/350a18c6-6b19-470d-adba-88c9e0394d0b/Right+Management+Flux+Report+Spread.pdf?MOD=AJPERES

[3] Clarke, R. (2016) *Over half of UK workers want to change careers*. Available at: www.hrreview.co.uk/hr-news/career-confusion-over-half-of-uk-workers-want-to-change-careers/60929

[4] No author. (2016) *Over Half of UK Workers Want To Change Career*. Available at: www.femalefirst.co.uk/money/over-half-of-uk-workers-want-to-change-career-913449.html

[5] Great Britain. Office for National Statistics. (2017) *Population by age, gender and ethnicity*. London, UK: Office for National Statistics. Available at: www.ons.gov.uk/aboutus/transparencyandgovernance/freedomofinformationfoi/populationbyagegenderandethnicity

[6] Dimock, M. (2018) *Defining generations: Where Millennials end and post-Millennials begin*. Available at: www.pewresearch.org/fact-tank/2018/03/01/defining-generations-where-millennials-end-and-post-millennials-begin/

[7] Great Britain. Office for National Statistics. (2018) *Number of People in Employment (aged 16 and over, seasonally adjusted)*. Available at: www.ons.gov.uk/employmentandlabourmarket/peopleinwork/employmentandemployeetypes/timeseries/mgrz/lms

[8] McGregor, J. (2013) *Only 13 percent of people worldwide actually like going to work*. (The Washington Post) Available at: www.washingtonpost.com/news/on-leadership/wp/2013/10/10/only-13-percent-of-people-worldwide-actually-like-going-to-work/?utm_term=.a93897d1490f

[9] Wells, J. (2015) *Is 'man up' the most destructive phrase in modern culture?* (The Telegraph) Available at: www.telegraph.co.uk/men/thinking-man/11724215/Is-man-up-the-most-destructive-phrase-in-modern-culture.html

[10] Chu, B. (2018) *UK employment at record high but real wages still falling, says ONS*. (The Independent) Available at: www.independent.co.uk/news/business/news/uk-employment-rate-high-real-wages-falling-ons-latest-statistics-a8175216.html

[11] Great Britain. Office for National Statistics. (2018) *Analysis of real earning: January 2018*. Available at: www.ons.gov.uk/employmentandlabourmarket/peopleinwork/earningsandworkinghours/articles/supplementaryanalysisofaverageweeklyearnings/january2018

[12] Dixon, A. (2016) *'Millennials' will spend £53,000 on rent by the time they turn 30*. (Zoopla) Available at: www.zoopla.co.uk/discover/property-news/so-called-millennials-pay-44-000-more-rent-by-the-time-they-reach-30-than-baby-boomers-says-resolution-foundation/#0Q9mSvYhytc3O3Ht.97

[13] Rudgard, O. (2018) *Millennials don't need living rooms, says leading architect.* (The Telegraph) Available at: www.telegraph.co.uk/news/2018/04/25/millennials-dont-need-living-rooms-says-leading-architect-says

[14] Pickford, J. (2017) *Bank of Mum and Dad is ninth-biggest lender with £6.5bn loans.* (The Financial Times) Available at: www.ft.com/content/0bd5e826-2e49-11e7-9555-23ef563ecf9a

[15] Murray, A. (2017) *The price I paid for borrowing £90,000 from the 'Bank of Mum and Dad'.* (The Telegraph) Available at: www.telegraph.co.uk/personal-banking/mortgages/price-paid-borrowing-90000-bank-mum-dad/

[16] Elliott, L & Osborne, H. (2016) *Under-35s in the UK face becoming permanent renters, warns thinktank.* (The Guardian) Available at: www.theguardian.com/society/2016/feb/13/under-35s-in-the-uk-face-becoming-permanent-renters-warns-thinktank

[17] Bennett, O. (2017) *Millennial Women Face Dramatic 'Pay Penalty' When They Become Mothers* (Huffington Post) Available at: www.huffingtonpost.co.uk/entry/millennial-women-face-dramatic-pay-penalty-when-they-become-mothers_uk_586bd0a9e4b0f24da6e9b14f

[18] Cosslett, R. (2017) *My generation has to choose between a child or a career. We can't afford both.* (The Guardian) Available at: www.theguardian.com/commentisfree/2017/apr/14/generation-child-career-afford-house-prices

[19] Newman, S. (2018) *Should We Worry About Millennials Not Having Babies?* (Psychology Today) Available at: www.psychologytoday.com/gb/blog/singletons/201804/should-we-worry-about-millennials-not-having-babies

[20] Durden, T. (2016) *Rent in London is Consuming 57% of Millennials' Income.* (ZeroHedge) Available at: www.zerohedge.com/news/2016-06-14/rent-london-consuming-57-millennials-income

[21] Percy, C & Mann, A. (2013) 'Employer Engagement in British Secondary Education: Wage Earning Outcomes Experienced by Young Adults', *Journal of Education and Work*, 27 (5).

[22] Great Britain. Department for Education. (2017) Careers strategy: making the most of everyone's skills and talents. London, UK: The Stationery Office. Available at: www.assets.publishing.service.gov.uk/government/uploads/system/uploads/attachment_data/file/664319/Careers_strategy.pdf

[23] News agencies. (2014) *Average women will kiss 15 men and be heartbroken twice before meeting 'The One', study reveals.* (The Telegraph) Available at: www.telegraph.co.uk/news/picturegalleries/howaboutthat/10545810/Average-woman-will-kiss-15-men-and-be-heartbroken-twice-before-meeting-The-One-study-reveals.html

[24] Ibid.

[25] Hosie, R. (2017) *How much British singletons spend on dating revealed.* (The Independent) Available at: www.independent.co.uk/life-style/love-sex/dating-british-single-relationships-drinks-foods-apps-a7639901.html

[26] Fisher, C. (2010) 'Happiness at work', International journal of management reviews, 12 (4), pp. 384-412. Available at: www.epublications.bond.edu.au/cgi/viewcontent.cgi?article=1307&context=business_pubs

[27] Mayo, E. (1932) 'The Human Problems of an Industrial Civilisation', Macmillan, 1933; 2nd edn Harvard University, 1946

[28] Hersey, R. B. (1932) *Workers' emotions in shop and home: A study of individual workers from the psychological and physiological standpoint-short title only in data base.* Philadelphia: University of Pennsylvania Press.

[29] Not everyone agrees with this. For a good summary, see: Spicer, A & Cederström, C. (2015) *The Research We've Ignored About Happiness at Work.* (Harvard Business Review) Available at: www.hbr.org/2015/07/the-research-weve-ignored-about-happiness-at-work

[30] No Author. (No date) *Resilience.* (Organisation Health Psychologists) Available at: www.orghealth.co.uk/resilience/resilient-workforce.html

[31] Harter, J & Schmidt, F. (2000) *Validation of a performance-related and actionable management tool: a meta-analysis and utility analysis* (Gallup Technical Report). Princeton, NJ: The Gallup Organization.

[32] Harter JK, Schmidt FL, Keyes CL (2003) Well-being in the workplace and its relationship to business outcomes: a review of the Gallup studies. In: Keyes CLM, Haidt J (eds) Flourishing: Positive Psychology and the Life Well-lived. Washington, DC: American Psychological Association, pp. 205-224.

[33] Piekałkiewicz, M. (2017) 'Why do economists study happiness?', *The Economic and Labour Relations Review,* 28 (3), pp. 361-377. Available at: www.doi.org/10.1177/1035304617717130

[34] Sgroi, D. (2015) Happiness and Productivity: Understanding the Happy-Productive Worker. SMF-CAGE Global Perspectives Series. Available at: www.warwick.ac.uk/fac/soc/economics/staff/dsgroi/impact/hp_briefing.pdf

[35] Hoxsey, D. (2010) 'Are happy employees healthy employees? Researching the effects of employee engagement on absenteeism', *The Institute of Public Administration of Canada.* Available at: www.onlinelibrary.wiley.com/doi/full/10.1111/j.1754-7121.2010.00148.x

[36] Nebeyou, A. (2015) 'The Value of Workplace Wellness Programs', *Employee Benefit Plan Review,* 70 (2), pp. 7-9.

[37] Phillips, C. (2016) 'A happier, healthier workplace', *New Hampshire Business Review,* 38(1), p. 24.

[38] Nowlan, K. Are happy employees healthier employees? Employee Assistance European Forum Autumn 2013. Available at: www.shepell.com/pdf/Are%20happy%20employees%20healthier%20employees.pdf

[39] Great Britain. Office for National Statistics. (2017) *Young adults living with their parents.* London, UK: Office for National Statistics. Available at: www.ons.gov.uk/peoplepopulationandcommunity/birthsdeathsandmarriages/families/datasets/youngadultslivingwiththeirparents

[40] Coughlan, S. (2016) *From boomers to stay-at-home boomerang generation.* (BBC) Available at: www.bbc.co.uk/news/education-36390999

[41] Watt, N, Wintour, P & Elliott, L. (2013) *State pension age to be raised to 70 for today's young workers.* (BBC) Available at: www.theguardian.com/uk-news/2013/dec/05/state-pension-age-raised-to-70-autumn-statement

[42] Montacute, R. (2018) Unpaid, Unadvertised, Unfair. (The Sutton Trust) Available at: www.suttontrust.com/research-paper/internships-unpaid-unadvertised-unfair

[43] Social Mobility and Child Poverty Commission. Great Britain. (2015) *A qualitative evaluation of non-educational barriers to the elite professions.* Available at: www.assets.publishing.service.gov.uk/government/uploads/system/uploads/attachment_data/file/434791/A_qualitative_evaluation_of_non-educational_barriers_to_the_elite_professions.pdf

[44] Malik, S. (2011) *Almost one in five British businesses admit using interns as cheap labour.* (The Guardian) Available at: www.theguardian.com/money/2011/apr/28/businesses-interns-cheap-labour

[45] Graduate Fog. (2015) *Can't find a graduate job? Perhaps you're just not posh enough.* Available at: www.graduatefog.co.uk/2015/4100/cant-find-a-graduate-job-perhaps-youre-just-not-posh-enough

[46] Great Britain. Office for National Statistics. (2017) *Graduates in the UK labour market: 2017.* Available at: www.ons.gov.uk/employmentandlabourmarket/peopleinwork/employmentandemployeetypes/articles/graduatesintheuklabourmarket/2017#graduates-and-non-graduates-in-work

[47] Great Britain. Department for Education. (No date) *Employment rights and pay for interns.* Available at: www.gov.uk/employment-rights-for-interns

[48] No author. (2016) *How Offering Work Experience To Young People Benefits Employers.* (E4S) Available at: recruiter.e4s.co.uk/2016/08/30/work-experience-young-people/

[49] I'Anson, J. (2012) *How to find unadvertised jobs.* (The Guardian) Available at: www.theguardian.com/careers/careers-blog/how-to-find-unadvertised-jobs

[50] Segelinm A. (2017) *3 Steps to Cracking the Hidden Job Market.* (Fortune) Available at: www.fortune.com/2017/03/04/hidden-job-market/

[51] Great Britain. Public Health England. (2016) *Green space, mental wellbeing and sustainable communities,* Available at: www.publichealthmatters.blog.gov.uk/2016/11/09/green-space-mental-wellbeing-and-sustainable-communities/

[52] Jenkin, M. (2016) *Written out of the story: the robots capable of making the news.* (The Guardian) Available at: www.theguardian.com/small-business-network/2016/jul/22/written-out-of-story-robots-capable-making-the-news

[53] Long, H. (2016) The new normal: 4 job changes by the time you're 32. (CNN Money) Available at: www.money.cnn.com/2016/04/12/news/economy/millennials-change-jobs-frequently

[54] No author. (2012) *What is portfolio working and why is it growing?* (The Telegraph) Available at: www.jobs.telegraph.co.uk/article/what-is-portfolio-working-and-why-is-it-growing-/

[55] Easterlin, R. A. (1974) 'Does economic growth improve the human lot? Some empirical evidence'. In: David, P & Melvin, W. (eds) *Nations and Households in Economic Growth*. Stanford, CA: Stanford University Press, pp. 98-125.

[56] Easterlin, R. A. (1995) 'Will raising the incomes of all increase the happiness of all?', Journal of Economic Behavior & Organization, 27 (1), pp. 35-47.

[57] Revesencio, J. (2015) *Why Happy Employees Are 12% More Productive*. (Fast Company) Available at: www.fastcompany.com/3048751/happy-employees-are-12-more-productive-at-work

[58] Wright, T & Staw, B. (1999) *Affect and Favorable Work Outcomes: Two Longitudinal Tests of the Happy-Productive Worker Thesis*, Journal of Organizational Behavior, 20 (1), pp. 1-23.

[59] Graham, C, Eggers, A & Sukhtankar, S. (2004) 'Does happiness pay? An exploration based on panel data from Russia', Journal of Economic Behavior & Organization, 55 (3), p. 336.

[60] Maslow, A. H. (1943) 'A Theory of Human Motivation', Psychological Review, 50, pp. 370-396.

[61] Maslow, A. H. (1987) 'Motivation and personality' (3rd ed.). Delhi, India: Pearson Education, p. 69.

[62] University of Southampton. (No date) *The benefits of a mentoring relationship*. Available at: www.southampton.ac.uk/professional-development/mentoring/benefits-of-a-mentoring-relationship.page

[63] Zimmerman, A. (2015) *Use a recent graduate as a career mentor and tap the millennial mindset*. (The Guardian) Available at: www.theguardian.com/women-in-leadership/2015/sep/10/recent-graduate-career-mentor-younger-generation

[64] No author. (No date) *What To Do When You Want To Do Everything: Is A Portfolio Career Right For You?* (Careershifters) Available at: www.careershifters.org/expert-advice/what-to-do-when-you-want-to-do-everything-could-a-portfolio-career-be-right-for-you

[65] *#GigResponsibly: The Rise of NextGen* Working report by ManpowerGroup (2017). Survey conducted by Three Group in November 2016 of 9,500 people across 12 countries including the UK who worked in both traditional and alternative ways.

[66] Waterman, R, Waterman, J & Collard, B. (1994) *Toward a Career-Resilient Workforce*. Harvard Business Review. Available at: www.hbr.org/1994/07/toward-a-career-resilient-workforce

[67] ManpowerGroup. (2017) *#GigResponsibly: The Rise of NextGen Working*. Available at: www.manpowergroup.com/wps/wcm/connect/cf010c08-826a-4f00-bd27-70a63144083d/manpowergroup-next-GEN-work.pdf?MOD=AJPERES

[68] Wallace, C. (2017) *Why Everyone Should Consider Building A Portfolio Career.* (Forbes) Available at: www.forbes.com/sites/christinawallace/2017/08/20/why-everyone-should-consider-building-a-portfolio-career/#7ec94602618d

[69] Right Management. (2014) 'The Flux Report: Building a resilient workforce in the face of flux'. ManpowerGroup. Available at: www.rightmanagement.co.uk/wps/wcm/connect/350a18c6-6b19-470d-adba-88c9e0394d0b/Right+Manageme nt+Flux+Report+Spread.pdf?MOD=AJPERES

[70] Schellenberg, B & Bailis, D. (2015) 'Can Passion be Polyamorous? The Impact of Having Multiple Passions on Subjective Well-Being and Momentary Emotions', Journal of Happiness Studies, 16 (16), pp. 1365-1381. Available at: www.link.springer.com/article/10.1007%2Fs10902-014-9564-x

[71] Hopson, B. (2018) *The Remote Working Model 2018.* (Portfolio Careers) Available at: www.portfoliocareers.net/2018/01/26/the-remote-working-model-2018/

[72] No author. (No date) *What To Do When You Want To Do Everything: Is A Portfolio Career Right For You?* (Careershifters) Available at: www. careershifters.org/expert-advice/what-to-do-when-you-want-to-do-everything-could-a-portfolio-career-be-right-for-you

[73] Spicer, A & Cederström, C. (2015) *The Research We've Ignored About Happiness At Work.* (Harvard Business Review) Available at: www.hbr. org/2015/07/the-research-weve-ignored-about-happiness-at-work

[74] Birch, C & Paul, D. (2003) *Life and work: Challenging economic man.* Sydney, Australia: UNSW Press.

[75] Wallace, C. (2017) *Why Everyone Should Consider Building A Portfolio Career.* (Forbes) Available at: www.forbes.com/sites/christinawallace/2017/08/20/why-everyone-should-consider-building-a-portfolio-career/#7ec94602618d

[76] Feldman, B. (2016) *BuzzFeed Reminds Its Employees: We Own Your Stuff.* (New York Magazine) Available at: www.nymag.com/selectall/2016/06/buzzfeed-reminds-its-employees-we-own-your-stuff.html

[77] Balaram, B. (2017) *Making the Gig Economy Work for Everyone.* (The RSA) Available at: www.thersa.org/discover/publications-and-articles/rsa-blogs/2017/04/making-the-gig-economy-work-for-everyone

[78] Balaram, B, Warden, J & Wallace-Stephens, F. (2017) *Good Gigs: A fairer future for the UK's gig economy.* (Medium) Available at: www.medium.com/rsa-reports/good-gigs-a-fairer-future-for-the-uks-gig-economy-f2485a22de09

[79] Hopson, B. (2017) *Portfolio careers and the Taylor report?* (Portfolio Careers) Available at: www.portfoliocareers.net/2017/07/12/portfolio-careers-and-the-taylor-report/comment-page-1/#comment-14910

[80] Great Britain. Office for National Statistics. (2018) *UK labour market: June 2018.* Available at: www.ons.gov.uk/employmentandlabourmarket/peopleinwork/employmentandemployeetypes/bulletins/uklabourmarket/june2018#young-people-in-the-labour-market

[81] Great Britain. Department for Work and Pensions. (2018) *Number in employment reaches record high.* Available at: www.gov.uk/government/news/number-in-employment-reaches-record-high

[82] Hoffman, R, Casnocha, B & Yeh, C. (2013) *Tours of Duty: The New Employer-Employee Contract.* (Harvard Business Review) Available at: www.hbr.org/2013/06/tours-of-duty-the-new-employer-employee-compact

[83] ManpowerGroup. (2017) *#GigResponsibly: The Rise of NextGen Working.* Available at: www.manpowergroup.com/wps/wcm/connect/cf010c08-826a-4f00-bd27-70a63144083d/manpowergroup-next-GEN-work.pdf?MOD=AJPERES

[84] Waterman, R, Waterman, J & Collard, B. (1994) *Toward a Career-Resilient Workforce.* Harvard Business Review. Available at: www.hbr.org/1994/07/toward-a-career-resilient-workforce

[85] Virgin. (No date) *In focus: The world's best start-up hubs.* Available at: www.virgin.com/entrepreneur/focus-worlds-best-start-hubs

[86] Hopson, B. (2018) *The Remote Working Model 2018.* (Portfolio Careers) Available at: www.portfoliocareers.net/2018/01/26/the-remote-working-model-2018/

[87] No author. (No date) *Know your rights.* (Freelancers in the UK) Available at: www.freelancersintheuk.co.uk/articles/know-your-rights/

[88] No author. (No date) *Self-employed.* (Acas) Available at: www.acas.org.uk/index.aspx?articleid=5890

[89] ManpowerGroup. (2017) *#GigResponsibly: The Rise of NextGen Working.* Available at: www.manpowergroup.com/wps/wcm/connect/cf010c08-826a-4f00-bd27-70a63144083d/manpowergroup-next-GEN-work.pdf?MOD=AJPERES

[90] Lunn, E. (2018) *Self-employed? Here's how to get a mortgage.* (The Guardian) Available at: www.theguardian.com/money/2018/feb/17/self-employed-mortgages-home-loans

[91] With thanks to Ronny Munster for his advice on this section.

APPENDICES

APPENDIX 1
CAREER ATTRIBUTES AND SKILLS

DEAL-BREAKERS	NICE-TO-HAVES

APPENDIX 2

CAREERS TO TRY: VERSION TWO

APPENDIX 3
CAREER ATTRIBUTES AND SKILLS
ANY CHANGES?

DEAL-BREAKERS	NICE-TO-HAVES

APPENDIX 4

Hunter S. Thompson was 22 years old when he wrote this letter to his friend Hume Logan who requested some life advice from Thompson, this features in the book Letter of Note: Correspondence Deserving of a Wider Audience.

April 22, 1958
57 Perry Street
New York City
Dear Hume,

...How does a man find a goal? Not a castle in the stars, but a real and tangible thing. How can a man be sure he's not after the 'big rock candy mountain', the enticing sugar-candy goal that has little taste and no substance?

The answer – and, in a sense, the tragedy of life – is that we seek to understand the goal and not the man. We set up a goal which demands of us certain things: and we do these things. We adjust to the demands of a concept which CANNOT be valid. When you were young, let us say that you wanted to be a fireman. I feel reasonably safe in saying that you no longer want to be a fireman. Why? Because your perspective has changed. It's not the fireman who has changed, but you. Every man is the sum total of his reactions to experience. As your experiences differ and multiply, you become a different man, and hence your perspective changes. This goes on and on. Every reaction is a learning process; every significant experience alters your perspective.

So it would seem foolish, would it not, to adjust our lives to the demands of a goal we see from a different angle every day? How could we ever hope to accomplish anything other than galloping neurosis?

The answer, then, must not deal with goals at all, or not with tangible goals, anyway. It would take reams of paper to develop this subject to fulfilment. God only knows how many books have been written on 'the meaning of man' and that sort of thing, and god only knows how many people have pondered the subject. (I use the term 'god only knows' purely as an expression.) There's very little sense in my trying to give it up to you in the proverbial nutshell, because I'm the first to admit my absolute lack of qualifications for reducing the meaning of life to one or two paragraphs.

To put our faith in tangible goals would seem to be, at best, unwise. So we do not strive to be firemen, we do not strive to be bankers, nor policemen, nor doctors. WE STRIVE TO BE OURSELVES.

But don't misunderstand me. I don't mean that we can't BE firemen, bankers, or doctors – but that we must make the goal conform to the individual, rather than make the individual conform to the goal. In every man, heredity and environment have combined to produce a creature of certain abilities and desires – including a deeply ingrained need to function in such a way that his life will be MEANINGFUL. A man has to BE something; he has to matter.

As I see it then, the formula runs something like this: a man must choose a path which will let his ABILITIES function at maximum efficiency toward the gratification of his DESIRES. In doing this, he is fulfilling a need (giving himself identity by functioning in a set pattern toward a set goal), he avoids frustrating his potential (choosing a path which puts no limit on his self-development), and he avoids the terror of seeing his goal wilt or lose its charm as he draws closer to it (rather than bending himself to meet the demands of that which he seeks, he has bent his goal to conform to his own abilities and desires).

In short, he has not dedicated his life to reaching a pre-defined goal, but he has rather chosen a way of life he KNOWS he will enjoy. The goal is absolutely secondary: it is the functioning toward the goal which is important. And it seems almost ridiculous to say that a man MUST function in a pattern of his own choosing; for to let another man define your own goals is to give up one of the most meaningful aspects of life – the definitive act of will which makes a man an individual.

Let's assume that you think you have a choice of eight paths to follow (all pre-defined paths, of course). And let's assume that you can't see any real purpose in any of the eight. THEN – and here is the essence of all I've said – you MUST FIND A NINTH PATH.

Naturally, it isn't as easy as it sounds. You've lived a relatively narrow life, a vertical rather than a horizontal existence. So it isn't any too difficult to understand why you seem to feel the way you do. But a man who procrastinates in his CHOOSING will inevitably have his choice made for him by circumstance.

So if you now number yourself among the disenchanted, then you have no choice but to accept things as they are, or to seriously seek something else. But beware of looking for goals: look for a way of life. Decide how you want to live and then see what you can do to make a living WITHIN that way of life. But you say, 'I don't know where to look; I don't know what to look for.'

And there's the crux. Is it worth giving up what I have to look for something better? I don't know – is it? Who can make that decision but you? But even by DECIDING TO LOOK, you go a long way toward making the choice.

Keep in mind, of course, that this is MY WAY of looking at things. I happen to think that it's pretty generally applicable, but you may not. Each of us has to create our own credo – this merely happens to be mine.

I'm not trying to send you out 'on the road' in search of Valhalla, but merely pointing out that it is not necessary to accept the choices handed down to you by life as you know it. There is more to it than that – no one HAS to do something he doesn't want to do for the rest of his life. But then again, if that's what you wind up doing, by all means convince yourself that you HAD to do it. You'll have lots of company.

And that's it for now. Until I hear from you again, I remain,
your friend,
Hunter S. Thompson